SpringerBriefs in Political Science

SpringerBriefs present concise summaries of cutting-edge research and practical applications across a wide spectrum of fields. Featuring compact volumes of 50 to 125 pages, the series covers a range of content from professional to academic. Typical topics might include:

- A timely report of state-of-the art analytical techniques
- A bridge between new research results, as published in journal articles, and a contextual literature review
- A snapshot of a hot or emerging topic
- An in-depth case study or clinical example
- A presentation of core concepts that students must understand in order to make independent contributions

SpringerBriefs in Political Science showcase emerging theory, empirical research, and practical application in political science, policy studies, political economy, public administration, political philosophy, international relations, and related fields, from a global author community.

SpringerBriefs are characterized by fast, global electronic dissemination, standard publishing contracts, standardized manuscript preparation and formatting guidelines, and expedited production schedules.

Dean Caivano

The Necro-President

Trump, MAGA, and the Decline of the American Republic

Dean Caivano
Department of Political Science
Lehigh University
Bethlehem, PA, USA

ISSN 2191-5466   ISSN 2191-5474 (electronic)
SpringerBriefs in Political Science
ISBN 978-3-031-94728-5   ISBN 978-3-031-94729-2 (eBook)
https://doi.org/10.1007/978-3-031-94729-2

© The Editor(s) (if applicable) and The Author(s) 2025. This book is an open access publication.

Open Access This book is licensed under the terms of the Creative Commons Attribution 4.0 International License (http://creativecommons.org/licenses/by/4.0/), which permits use, sharing, adaptation, distribution and reproduction in any medium or format, as long as you give appropriate credit to the original author(s) and the source, provide a link to the Creative Commons license and indicate if changes were made.
The images or other third party material in this book are included in the book's Creative Commons license, unless indicated otherwise in a credit line to the material. If material is not included in the book's Creative Commons license and your intended use is not permitted by statutory regulation or exceeds the permitted use, you will need to obtain permission directly from the copyright holder.
The use of general descriptive names, registered names, trademarks, service marks, etc. in this publication does not imply, even in the absence of a specific statement, that such names are exempt from the relevant protective laws and regulations and therefore free for general use.
The publisher, the authors and the editors are safe to assume that the advice and information in this book are believed to be true and accurate at the date of publication. Neither the publisher nor the authors or the editors give a warranty, expressed or implied, with respect to the material contained herein or for any errors or omissions that may have been made. The publisher remains neutral with regard to jurisdictional claims in published maps and institutional affiliations.

This Springer imprint is published by the registered company Springer Nature Switzerland AG.
The registered company address is: Gewerbestrasse 11, 6330 Cham, Switzerland

If disposing of this product, please recycle the paper.

The messianic is not the end of time, but the time of the end.
Giorgio Agamben

The earth belongs to the living, not to the dead.
Thomas Jefferson

Preface

The premise of this book is simple: the American presidency represents the paradigmatic figure of life. The executive's central function is to exert a life force strong enough to delay, if not overpower, the encroachments of death upon the republic.

The president is, in this schema, life incarnate—a figure that embodies executive authority and the vitality of the republic. But the continuity of that symbolism has begun to unravel. It has been threatened by the alarming suggestion that death has penetrated the very walls of the executive. The supposed immortality of the office—and its occupant—is false and actively being undone. The illusion has shattered. The appearance of one mortal figure has announced the mortality of the republic itself, exposing rupture points in the architecture of governance. Death has crossed the Rubicon, and the symbolic order of the republic is now adrift in the abyss of postmodernity.

What conditions could summon such an existential crisis? This book seeks to provide an answer.

The presidential election of 2024 lies at the heart of this inquiry. What emerged was atypical from the all-too-familiar theatrics of partisan disputes. Instead, the sitting president, Joseph R. Biden, came to be seen not merely as ineffective or faltering but as something far more insidious: *dead*. His image was transformed from that of adiminished leader into a symbol of presidential mortality itself.

With death seated in the White House, the collapse of the republic appeared forthcoming. But through an unexpected twist of political dramaturgy, a crusader cloaked in the vestments of vitality and divine appointment seized the election and promised to reverse the course of impending doom. Such a reframing made Donald J. Trump's triumph possible.

Trump became *the* resurrection of the presidency: the defeat of the *dead president*, the *necro-president*, and enabling the restoration of America. And yet, as the pages that follow will suggest, this conquering of death did not yield the triumph of life. Quite the opposite; it secured the victory of death over life. What remains is not the temporary exile of the necro-president but rather the election of it.

This book argues that the necro-president is not just a label attached to a singular political actor, Biden in this case, or a partisan character of disdain. Instead, a conceptual and symbolic condition illuminates the tension between vitality and decay within the American political tradition. In the chapters that follow, I draw a distinction between two modes of presidential death: *Biden as entropy*, a figure of passive decline who embodies the exhaustion and collapse of institutional life, and *Trump as necro-sovereign*, a figure who mobilizes death actively, consolidating power through spectacle, fascistic energy, and the promise of permanent survival *qua* domination. Throughout this work, I will sketch out critical facets of this symbolic crisis, tracing the theoretical foundations of republican decay, the role of succession and death, the emergence of political spectacle, and the cultural aftermath of collapse.

I wrote this book to make sense of what I was seeing (discourses of dehumanization, erosion of public institutions, violence against marginalized groups) and feeling (powerlessness, grief, mourning). As a political theorist, I kept returning to the question of what it means when symbolic power fails and, in turn, when an institution designed to represent vitality begins to collapse under the weight of its mortality and contradictions. As an educator, I engaged with students trying to grasp the meaning of a system—and future—that increasingly feels lifeless, hollowed out, and unsustainable.

The following pages take these institutional, symbolic, and spiritual crises seriously as a symptom of something deeper: the decay of symbolic life in American political culture. This is not a book about the death of American democracy. It is a book about what remains when political symbols keep circulating long after their animating force has faded.

Bethlehem, PA, USA   Dean Caivano

Acknowledgments

Thanks to the anonymous reviewers of this manuscript. Their close readings and thoughtful feedback helped clarify the stakes of this project, and I'm grateful for the time and care they gave it.

At Lehigh University, I've been lucky to work alongside generous and thoughtful colleagues in the Department of Political Science. I'm especially thankful to Nandini Deo, Anthony DiMaggio, and Marie Schenk for their steady support, honest conversations, and good humor throughout the writing process. Our weekly writing sessions in the Commons became a space of community, creativity, and routine that helped carry this work forward.

I'm also grateful to the College of Arts and Sciences at Lehigh for supporting my research and to Nicholas Pesarcik for helping me navigate funding questions to make Open-Access publication possible.

The students in my Politics of Despair seminar have played an ongoing role in shaping my thoughts about this project. Their willingness to wrestle with complex texts and ask meaningful questions influenced the development of this work.

Finally, to Sarah Naumes, thank you for tactfully and graciously encouraging me to pursue this book's central idea.

Competing Interests The author has no competing interests to declare that are relevant to the content of this manuscript.

Contents

1   A Thousand Unexpected Ways 1
2   Wither Republic 7
3   To Keep the Republic 21
4   The Necro-President 39
5   Pace Death 57

About the Author

Dean Caivano is a political theorist specializing in American political thought and radical democracy. He is an assistant professor in the Department of Political Science at Lehigh University. His books include *A Politics of All: Thomas Jefferson and Radical Democracy* (Lexington Books, 2023) and *The Sublime of the Political: Narrative & Autoethnography as Theory* (transcript Verlag & Columbia University Press, 2021). His scholarship has also appeared in various academic journals, including *Philosophy & Social Criticism*, *New Political Science*, and the *Journal of Narrative Politics*.

Chapter 1
A Thousand Unexpected Ways

The womb is fertile still from which this monster crawled.
Bertolt Brecht

Abstract I introduce the concept of the necro-president as a figure and condition that emerges at the intersection of institutional decay, symbolic death, and political myth. Framed through the 2024 presidential election, I argue that Joseph R. Biden functions as entropy, a spectral embodiment of decline, while Donald J. Trump operates as necro-sovereign. This figure reclaims decay through spectacle and mythic restoration. Drawing from the republican tradition's concern with fragility and collapse, I show how the presidency has shifted from a symbol of vitality to a vessel of exhaustion. The necro-president offers a lens for theorizing the unraveling of symbolic authority and the transformation of executive power during political decline.

Keywords Necro-president · Republican decay · 2024 election · Symbolic authority · Trumpism · Biden · Executive power · Political myth · Institutional collapse

On January 1, 2025, two acts of violence illustrated the fragile state of the American republic. These were not isolated incidents but stark manifestations of deeper institutional decay and existential threat. In New Orleans, Shamsud-Din Jabbar, a 42-year-old Army veteran who had served in Afghanistan, launched a truck attack, killing fifteen and injuring dozens (Winter et al., 2025). Hours later, across the country in Las Vegas, Matthew Alan Livelsberger, an active-duty Green Beret, orchestrated a suicidal explosion outside Trump Tower. Investigators found messages on Livelsberger's phone linking his act to the belief that the United States was "headed toward collapse," a fate only legible through "spectacle and violence" (Fortin et al., 2025). These events underscore the republic's growing susceptibility to fragmentation and crisis.

Unexpected Ways Abound Republican theory has long grappled with such fragility. Shaped by pessimistic insights, the tradition of republican thought holds that institutional decay and collapse are inevitable. In his *Discourses on Livy*, Machiavelli offers a cautionary maxim: "It is impossible to order a perpetual republic because its ruin is caused through a thousand unexpected ways" (1996, p. 257). Rather than aspiring to permanence, republican theorists have historically sought to delay collapse through mechanisms that cultivate virtue, institutional renewal, and civic stability (Caivano, 2023). Yet, even these efforts can only forestall, not prevent, the inevitable decline.

As the American republic approaches its quarter-millennium mark, Machiavelli's insight feels especially prescient. From the erosion of institutional trust to the normalization of political violence and extremist ideologies, the promise of American exceptionalism seems increasingly suspect. While historians often point to economic inequality, imperial overreach, and democratic backsliding as root causes, these analyses frequently miss the more subtle, symbolic terrain where political meaning erodes—where language, images, and collective psychology begin to fall apart.

The MAGA movement's claim that the 2020 election was stolen heightened the stakes of the 2024 rematch between Donald J. Trump and Joseph R. Biden. The election appeared beyond the gravity of an electoral contest but a struggle over the future of the republic. For MAGA supporters, a Trump victory offered an opportunity for procedural revisionism and, most importantly, an opening for a temporal restoration that would purify the present, redeem the past, and project certainty into the future.

Critically, while Biden campaigned on a platform to save democracy, Trump took a markedly different approach. Trump crusaded on a plan to save the American republic. His campaign did not rely merely on policy proposals or culture-war grievances. It was powered by something more primal: anxiety about collapse. Biden and eventual Democratic Party nominee Kamala Harris were cast as proxies for a system already in decay. At the heart of this staging was Biden himself, spectral and slow, transformed into a ghostly emblem of institutional death.

That figure—what I offer here as a conceptual framework is the *necro-president*—signals the symbolic and structural collapse of executive authority. The necro-president isn't a descriptor of an aging or ineffective executive. It speaks to a condition of the political scene where death shapes the contours of the American political imaginary. In MAGA rhetoric, the necro-president is both a symptom and a threat, haunting the executive branch and rendering weakness into a metaphysical crisis. It articulates a symbolic condition in which the presidency no longer coheres as a source of vitality or national meaning. Instead, it becomes saturated with death.

This book traces two manifestations of this condition: *Biden as entropy*, the slow drift into institutional silence, and *Trump as necro-sovereign*, a figure who animates death through spectacle and political myth. The necro-president, then, is not just a label. I want to offer it as a theoretical lens for understanding how symbolic authority has collapsed and been repurposed in the wake of decay.

The theory of the necro-president contains a double meaning: it is *figure* and *condition*. It marks a shift in how the presidency is symbolically, rhetorically, and ontologically represented. In deploying the concept, I seek to show how it moves across registers of thought from its symbolic weight, marking a shift from projections of vitality to vacancy to its rhetorical force, capturing how the language of death within our political imagination to finally, how ontologically undoing, suggestive of a deeper unraveling in the meaning of the office itself. What was once the living center of the republic has become a hollowed-out shell. The necro-president gives shape to that transformation.

The spirit of the necro-president, as figure and concept, inadvertently was articulated by Trump's disciple, Andy Ogles, a Republican Congressman from Tennessee. A mere three days following the start of Trump's second term, Ogles presented a resolution to amend the 22nd Amendment to the Constitution to "give President Trump a third term!" (Ogles, 2025) While it's easy to dismiss Ogles's efforts as sycophant grandeur par excellence, the justification offered as to why a third term is warranted cuts to the heart of the necro-presidency. Amending the constitution is an imperative precisely because, as Ogles offers, "He [Trump] has proven himself to be the only figure in modern history capable of reversing our nation's decay and restoring America to greatness, and he must be given the time necessary to accomplish that goal" (Vigdor, 2025). Political theater? Absolutely. Yet, the proposed resolution and discursive justification also contain a critical impulse of the representative power of Trump, the figure, and the concept.

Building on Machiavelli's warnings, I situate the emergence of the necro-president within a broader genealogy of republican decay. Under Trump's leadership, the MAGA movement has intensified perceptions of collapse, invoking threats both external and internal: the "enemy within" (Cooper, 2024), "animals" and "not human" (Layneet al., 2024), and immigrants from "shithole countries" (Desjardins, 2018). These designations don't just define enemies but carry with them a perspective that the republic is corrupted nearly-beyond repair and that only a messianic force can cleanse it. In this framework, Trump is not merely a candidate. He is the redeemer.

Making sense of this symbolic unraveling, I draw from conceptions of death, decay, and fascism framed not as endpoints but as active political conditions. The necro-president resonates with Hannah Arendt's reflections on mortality and collective life. "Our own death," she writes, "is accompanied by the potential immortality of the group we belong to" (1970, p. 68). Arendt believed this awareness could galvanize action. The necro-president reverses that logic. Death is no longer the condition for renewal—it becomes the governing principle. It accelerates what Jack Balkin (2017, 2018) calls constitutional rot, a hollowing out of institutional life that masks itself in legitimacy. In this configuration, the presidency becomes not a symbol of regeneration but a vessel of exhaustion.

As Jason Stanley (2018) argues, the erosion of democratic norms results from a deliberate strategy that relies on emotion, fear, and repetition. Jodi Dean (2009) shows us how communicative excess can actually undermine democratic life when a political field becomes oversaturated with images, affect, and information. The consequence is not the recognition of political consensus as an order but an acceleration of fraught circulation. And as Anthony DiMaggio (2022) makes clear, the diagnoses offered by Stanley, Dean, and others miss the full implication of the current order. For DiMaggio, our current political moment does not indicate a passive, slow drift away from norms but an organized project. In this way, the collapse of democratic institutions must be seen as engineered by elite actors who manipulate disaffection, provoke crisis, and deploy fascist rhetoric and policies to consolidate power. These thinkers help situate the necro-president beyond the realm of description; instead, they provide a way to explore the symbolic condition of a broader authoritarian logic that thrives on collapse.

This Is the Political World that the Necro-President Inhabits The 2024 election, framed as a referendum on republican survival, reveals how symbolic death justified procedural rupture. Biden's perceived frailty became the logic for redemption. The necro-president operates as a kind of symbolic summarization of the necropolitical. Where the necropolitical, in my perspective, refers to a mode of governance that deploys death as a strategy, the necro-president is the executive embodiment of its logic. This figure doesn't just preside over decay but animates it as an inescapable condition of political life. Trump's ascent exploits fears of institutional breakdown, marking death as a logic of governance. If Biden embodies entropy, Trump reclaims that perceived stillness, silence, and decay and regenerates it through spectacle, vengeance, and mythic restoration. Death becomes no longer a limit but a condition of power.

If we accept Machiavelli's warning that republics fall through a thousand unexpected ways, perhaps then we may conclude that we are living in the most surprising times. A regime climax that avoids collapse through war or external forces but declines by a leader who claims *victory over death itself*. However, for Trump, the presidency has ascended to a plane of immorality, eschewing the fragility of the republic and enacting a new horizon that is mythic, eternal, and purified by his dominion. Power calcifies in that delusion of vitality, in the refusal to mourn what has already collapsed. Trump is not just inside the necropolitical frame. *He is its sovereign, architect, and ultimate expression.*

The following pages examine this claim. In Chap. 2, I turn to the republican tradition to explore the persistence of fears about decay and the evolved institutional responses to address these anxieties. The responses crafted as safeguards have been exhausted, leaving a specter of erosion that necessitates acknowledgment. I then, in Chap. 3, focus on one of the most significant strategies operationalized within the republican universe to slow inevitable collapse: the promise of leadership continuity. Chapter 4 takes us from the fractured line of presidential succession into the spectacle of the 2024 election, where death becomes staged, memed, mythologized, and turned into doctrine. Trump doesn't just return; he ascends—not as a man, but as a sovereign immune to decay. Finally, in Chap. 5, I reject the idea the necropolitical order warrants a configuration of politics aiming at national redemption, or terroristic revolt, or even a descent into nihilism. The question isn't how to save the republic but what can be done from within its ongoing collapse. Taking seriously Arendt's claim that death moves to the center of collective experience, I argue that we must *act with death*. The task before us is thus a recognition of *existence within collapse*, which demands an inquiry into what, if anything at all, might still be possible within the institutional, symbolic, and spiritual necropolis of our collective ruins.

References

Arendt, H. (1970). *On violence*. Harcourt, Brace & World.
Balkin, J. M. (2017). Constitutional crisis and constitutional rot. *Maryland Law Review, 77*(1), 151.
Balkin, J. M. (2018). Constitutional rot. In C. R. Sunstein (Ed.), *Can it happen here? Authoritarianism in America* (pp. 19–36). HarperCollins.
Caivano, D. (2023). *A politics of all: Thomas Jefferson and radical democracy*. Lexington Books.
Cooper, J. J. (2024, October 26). Who does Trump see as 'enemies from within'? *AP News*. https://apnews.com/article/donald-trump-enemies-from-within-5c4a34776469a55e71d3ba4d4e68cf62
Dean, J. (2009). *Democracy and other neoliberal fantasies: Communicative capitalism and left politics*. Duke University Press.
Desjardins, L. (2018, January 15). Did Trump say 'shithole'? Who said what about what Trump said. *PBS NewsHour*. https://www.pbs.org/newshour/politics/did-trump-say-shole-who-said-what-about-what-trump-said
DiMaggio, A. R. (2022). *Rising fascism in America: It can happen here*. Routledge.
Fortin, J., Philipps, D., & Jiménez, J. (2025, January 3). Soldier in Tesla blast had PTSD and feared U.S. 'collapse,' officials say. *The New York Times*. https://www.nytimes.com/2025/01/03/us/las-vegas-tesla-explosion-soldier-ptsd-notes.html
Layne, N., Slattery, G., & Reid, T. (2024, April 3). Trump calls migrants 'animals,' intensifying focus on illegal immigration. *Reuters*. https://www.reuters.com/world/us/trump-expected-highlight-murder-michigan-woman-immigration-speech-2024-04-02/
Machiavelli, N. (1996). In H. Mansfield (Ed.), *Discourses on livy*. University of Chicago Press.
Ogles, A. (2025, January 23). Rep. Ogles proposes amending 22nd Amendment to allow Trump to serve third term [Press release]. U.S. House of Representatives. https://ogles.house.gov/media/press-releases/rep-ogles-proposes-amending-22nd-amendment-allow-trump-serve-third-term
Stanley, J. (2018). *How fascism works: The politics of us and them*. Random House.
Vigdor, N. (2025, March 31). No, Trump Cannot Run for Re-election Again in 2028. *The New York Times*. https://www.nytimes.com/2024/11/18/us/politics/trump-third-term.html
Winter, T., et al. (2025, January 3). The driver in the New Orleans attack was an Army veteran from Texas. *NBC News*. https://www.nbcnews.com/news/us-news/law-enforcement-officials-identify-suspect-new-orleans-attack-rcna185929

Open Access This chapter is licensed under the terms of the Creative Commons Attribution 4.0 International License (http://creativecommons.org/licenses/by/4.0/), which permits use, sharing, adaptation, distribution and reproduction in any medium or format, as long as you give appropriate credit to the original author(s) and the source, provide a link to the Creative Commons license and indicate if changes were made.

The images or other third party material in this chapter are included in the chapter's Creative Commons license, unless indicated otherwise in a credit line to the material. If material is not included in the chapter's Creative Commons license and your intended use is not permitted by statutory regulation or exceeds the permitted use, you will need to obtain permission directly from the copyright holder.

Chapter 2
Wither Republic

> *The corruption will increase among the corruptors...*
>
> *Montesquieu*

Abstract I examine how republican theory, both classical and contemporary, wrestles with the inevitability of decay. I argue that two existential conditions define the republican project: institutional inevitability and procedural contingency. These twin logics reflect the awareness of regime mortality and the design of mechanisms intended to delay collapse. Drawing from a rich tradition of thinkers, including Aristotle, Augustine, Machiavelli, Rousseau, and Madison, I trace how decline is encoded into republican architecture, from ancient succession planning to modern fears of populism and institutional rot. This chapter reframes republicanism not as a solution to crisis, but as a system built to manage it, a structure of ephemeral permanence calibrated to metabolize corruption, failure, and mortality. I show how neoliberalism, authoritarian nostalgia, and spectacle politics have eroded these stabilizing devices, making space for the necro-president to emerge, not as a rupture but as a symptom of the republican body's exhaustion.

Keywords Republican theory · Institutional decay · Constitutional design · Neoliberalism · Populism · Succession planning · Institutional resilience · Governance crisis

This chapter traces how classical and contemporary theorists grapple with the inevitability of republican decay and ruin. These inherent existential tensions manifest in theory and institutional design, which I conceptualize as two fundamental conditions of republican governance: *institutional inevitability* and *procedural contingency*. Both are central to understanding the history of republican theory and the present crisis of the American republic.

The inevitability of decay and the ruin of the body politic are central themes in the canon of Western political thought. Plato's regime classification outlines a cyclical deterioration of political bodies and their corresponding transformation into defective forms. Montesquieu's *Persian Letters* (1973), an epistolary novel with significant political undertones, posits that political bodies are always vulnerable to decay, thrust upon an accelerated path when the ancestral past is repressed. Accordingly, a crucial component of citizenship is thus to preserve and keep the past alive, projecting it into the present and future to sustain the body politic. In *On the Social Contract* (1986a, pp. 149–221) and his unfinished *Constitutional Project for Corsica* (1986b, pp. 279–321), Jean-Jacques Rousseau stresses an unavoidable devolution of a body politic, which begins at its very moment of conception. Rousseau cautions that separating the political body from an institutional arrangement of power almost certainly expedites the processes of decline and decay, resulting in, unmistakenly and unavoidably, collapse.

2.1 Decline, Decay, & Collapse: Then and Now

Ancient and early modern thinkers equated regime decline with diminishing civic virtue, pervasive corruption, and the repression of founding principles. Montesquieu, for instance, observed that "the corruption of every government generally begins with that of its principles" (2002, p. 109). In a monarchy, honor is diverted into vanity; in a despotism, fear gives way to ridicule; and in a republic, virtue is displaced by private interest. As Näsström and Kalm (2015) note, these transformations may leave a regime's outer structures intact while hollowing them out from within, reducing institutions to "empty vessels of a bygone time" (562). In this way, corruption does not strictly appear as institutional collapse but as symbolic and ethical erosion. Camila Vergara (2021) insightfully underscores the destructive impact of corruption in ancient regimes, reflecting individual political actors' unethical behavior and serving as a broader indication of systemic issues. Vergara (2022) shows how the normalization of corruption reveals structural deficiencies that create conditions for institutional decay and ineffective governance.

Contemporary theorists have also offered valuable accounts. Emphasizing a premise centered on the effects of civic deterioration in institutional and citizenship contexts, recent analyses have highlighted how economic forces have eclipsed political power, posing a significant threat to the vitality of republican governance. For Sheldon Wolin (2017), the rise of corporate power directly undermines democratic institutions and participatory spaces, culminating in what he terms "inverted totalitarianism." Like Näsström and Kalm, Wolin sketches out a system in which democratic structures exist in form but are hollowed out in practice, functioning as corporate-managed entities devoid of genuine popular control. Similarly, Wendy Brown (2015) critiques neoliberalism's inherent logic, which reduces all domains of social life to quantifiable economic terms (41). Brown argues that neoliberal rationality has transformed the political essence of freedom into an economic form

(37–40). With the erasure of active, politically engaged citizens, individuals are reduced to the figure of *homo oeconomicus*, resulting in the undermining of democratic norms and institutions and the depletion of political energies from public life.[1]

In her recent work, Brown (2019) reflects on how neoliberalism has mutated beyond its foundational dictates of privatization and marketization, grafting itself onto Christian morality, prominently on display in the United States (115–122). This fusion of traditional, reactionary moralism with a neoliberal economic agenda is concurrent with Margaret Thatcher's infamous proclamation that "there is no such thing as society" through a rejection of liberal orthodoxy in favor of a tribalist understanding of self and family. Brown links this shift in neoliberal rationality to mainstream ascendancy and policy influence as a consequence of the ardent support of evangelical Christians for President Trump. Brown suggests that this confluence of neoliberalism and evangelical moralism deepens societal erosion, signaling a nihilistic outlook that is now promulgated by technocrats and evangelicals.

Wolin and Brown's diagnoses, which focus on the dual institutional and civic unraveling of democracy, acquire conceptual depth when placed alongside thinkers such as Chantal Mouffe and Cornel West. Mouffe (2005a, 2005b) critiques the rise of technocratic governance in reducing life to a depoliticized, economized framework of interaction and exclusion (146). Offering a warning, Mouffe cautions against the growing tendency to eliminate structured institutional-based conflict à la Machiavelli's *Discourses* in favor of attaining consensus. According to Mouffe, the effect erodes pluralistic and contestatory frameworks necessary for a vibrant democracy (2013, pp. 103–114). In this post-political paradigm, contestation becomes obsolete, replaced by an impulse for uniformity and enclosure.

West shares similar concerns about the erosion of civic life, underscoring the homogenizing demands of neoliberal capitalism. West rebukes the commodification of all aspects of life, exacerbating economic inequality and concentrating wealth and power in fewer hands. He further identifies the repercussions of these dynamics: declining trust, unraveling forms of accountability, and ineffectiveness effectiveness. But West's critique extends beyond the material. He contends that a deeper ontological decay sets in when political institutions deteriorate and inequality intensifies. This decay, he argues, permeates from the corridors of power to collective and individual spirituality (West 2014, p. 67). As nihilism spreads, material wealth and personal success precede values like care, empathy, and community (West 2005, p. 40). In a sobering yet decisively nondeterministic outlook, West warns that institutional decline and collective uncertainty foster individual despair, driving the need for a qualitatively different vision of the future.

The affinities among Wolin, Brown, Mouffe, and West are striking. Their assessments also resonate with the work of Jacques Rancière (1999, 2007), who similarly

---

[1] The term *homo oeconomicus* refers to the theoretical figure of a rational, self-interested economic agent, often criticized for reducing human behavior to market logics. For a rich exploration, see Michel Foucault's *The Birth of Biopolitics* (2008), where he traces the emergence of *homo oeconomicus* in neoliberal governance. Wendy Brown also offers a sharp critique in *Undoing the Demos* (2015), examining how this figure has come to displace democratic subjectivity altogether.

critiques governance structures, which are representative and thus inherently oligarchic, stripped of active input from the political community.[2] Collectively, they expose how the erosion of civic engagement and the hollowing out of democratic institutions is devastating. Their critiques converge on depicting a democratic society in name only, drained of robust expressions of citizenship and productive institutionalized conflict, mutated into a precariously functioning, decaying post-democratic state.

Scholars have thus sounded the alarm over the erosion of democratic norms and institutions and the diminishing adherence to principles of republican governance. In the context of the American republic, these critiques underscore the profound challenges posed by neoliberalism, economic inequality, and the commodification of civic life, painting a dire portrait of a polity in crisis.

Tracing the erosion of American democracy from the 1980s to the present, Levitsky and Ziblatt (2018) argue that unwritten norms, particularly mutual toleration and forbearance, are being strikingly disregarded. Although the American political system has undoubtedly endured previous crises, Levitsky and Ziblatt stress that the abandonment of these democratic norms threatens the Madisonian system. Moreover, they isolate extreme partisanship, further exacerbated by Trump, as a critical factor weakening the "guardrails of American democracy" (9).

Likewise, Anne Applebaum, in *Twilight of Democracy: The Seductive Lure of Authoritarianism* (2020), explores the perilous state of Western democracies due to the rise of authoritarian movements across Europe and the United States. The erosion of democratic norms and institutions—historically sustained, deepened, and expanded in the United States through the republican design—is multifaceted. Notably, Applebaum pays attention to how nostalgia penetrates and destabilizes the legitimacy of democracy. Drawing an important distinction between reflective nostalgia—a sense of memorializing the past without seeking to recreate its conditions in the present—and restorative nostalgia, Applebaum argues that the latter poses a critical threat (cf. ch. III). Accordingly, restorative nostalgia deploys half-baked ideas linked to vague, broad themes, such as greatness or patriotism, to critique present configurations of governmental authority and the constitutive forces of civic engagement.

Fundamental to disseminating restorative nostalgia discourses is the role of hyper-partisan news and political outlets that exploit and deepen distrust in democratic norms among their adherents. As the reliability and credibility of formerly widely accepted traditional news platforms fade, the ubiquity of counter-narratives accelerates through constant repetition, fermenting further levels of distrust. The effects are profound, including destabilizing mutual understandings around claims of truth and objectivity. Albeit always incomplete, objectivity and truth give way to erroneous narratives or even conspiratorial claims (cf. ch. IV). These

---

[2] Martin Breaugh and Dean Caivano discuss the treatment of the erosion of democratic-republican norms among prominent democratic theorists, highlighting how the conceptual framing of "post-democracy" provides much-needed analytical clarity for contextualizing institutional and civic deterioration (2024).

counter-narratives, laden with lies, deception, and conspiracy theories, become weaponized to instrumentalize pessimistic messaging about the decline of society.

For Applebaum, far-right politics and Trump exemplify efforts to tap into restorative nostalgia, infusing it into rhetoric, party platforms, and governance. Applebaum's analysis is of significant use for our exploration of the necro-president, revealing how authoritarianism undermines democratic norms and legitimacy. Moreover, Applebaum highlights how truth has become subordinated to power. The validity of claims within an ideological paradigm that clamors for the resurrection of the past becomes meaningless. Instead, their discursive weight is revealed precisely through extraordinary, embellished assertions. The further these claims deviate from mutually accepted forms of objectivity, the more impactful they become among followers as a form of social currency against the status quo establishment.

Yascha Mounk's analysis, too, offers a somber assessment of the precipitous erosion of liberal democratic norms and institutions. In *The People* vs. *Democracy: Why Our Freedom is in Danger and How to Save It* (2018), Mounk provides analytical clarity by distinguishing between liberalism—institutions designed to "ensure the rule of law and guarantee individual rights" (27)—and democracy, the mechanism through which majority rule is translated into public policy via established electoral institutions. While the conceptual parameters of these terms remain deeply rooted in an institutionalist perspective—to the point that arguably negates democracy's ontological foundation of equality—Mounk's delineation of terms is an important and helpful reminder. Drawing careful distinctions helps avoid the analytical conflation of terms and the discursive tendency to "smuggle all desirable qualities into the very notion of democracy" (26). This point is paramount, as Mounk reminds us that democracy, as a system of governance, can indeed become illiberal.

Mounk maintains that when liberalism and democracy are conjoined, the result is a stable, institutionalized framework *for* liberal democracy. However, the rise of right-wing populism has severed this linkage. Reactionary populist leaders, critical of liberal democratic values and institutions, exploit public discontent, channeling frustrations into an energetic assault against political elites and established norms. In the United States and across Europe, Mounk observes a discernable decline in trust in government. This development threatens democratic stability as populists further attempt to undermine the very institutions they seek to capture.

One of the most prominent clarion calls forewarning the specter of authoritarianism and fascism in Western democracies is found in Timothy Snyder's *On Tyranny* (2017). Using the twentieth century as a tableau, Snyder distills key lessons to identify the antecedent conditions that enabled the decimation of the public and social realms, accelerating the rise of authoritarian tendencies. From advocating for the defense of institutions to rejecting one-party dominance and resisting false narratives, Snyder emphasizes the fragility of democratic institutions and the ease with which they can deteriorate into illiberal forms.

While Snyder offers a gloomy prognosis of authoritarian creep unfolding among Western governments, his work is counterbalanced by a call for vigilance and careful historical inquiry. In a moment of exceptional clarity, Snyder reminds us that history—much like republican theory—is *not* inherently on the side of democracy. The history of modern democracies, he argues, is a story of decline and collapse, echoing a warning long ago articulated by Machiavelli (1998). Reflecting on the rise of communism and fascism and addressing America's misplaced sense of immunity, Snyder writes, "We might be tempted to think that our democratic heritage automatically protects us from such threats. This is a misguided reflex" (2017, p. 8). As the moral, institutional, and cultural fibers of liberal democracy continue to unravel, Snyder's work offers critical insight: when the centrifugal forces of governance weaken, governance itself increasingly centers on death, decay, and the reanimation of exclusionary ideals. Snyder's analysis thus serves as both a historical warning and a contemporary call to action to defend the tenuous institutions of democracy before they are irrevocably undone.

These assessments, from Plato to Brown to Snyder, underscore the importance of institutional design in republican theory *then and now*. The survival and flourishing of a republic hinge on how effectively its institutions and citizens can regulate the forces of decay to preserve the regime and develop mechanisms to extend its lifespan. The republican tradition offers a range of strategies to stabilize a regime—separation of powers, accountable representation, and adherence to the rule of law. These mechanisms aim to prevent political corruption and moral decay, preserving institutional functionality.

Yet if our survey has illuminated the consequences of republican decline, how might we distill the deeper structures that either delay or accelerate collapse? To answer this, we must turn back to Machiavelli's insight about the cyclical nature of all governments from their inception to their inevitable demise (1996, p. 13). Republican design, at its core, wrestles with two fundamental conditions that respond to the corrosive effects of time and human agency. These conditions—institutional inevitability and procedural contingency—represent the twin pillars of republican theory. They speak not only to the functioning of governmental departments but also to the architectural and temporal strategies created to preserve the foundational principles of the republic.

2.2 Two Existential Conditions of the Republican Body Politic

Republican theory is a project of careful calibration, revealing the symbiotic relationship between politics and architecture—constructing structures of ephemeral permanence for inhabitation. Inhabitation, here, refers to creating a system where individuals collaborate with humanly designed, inanimate structures to impede corruption and abuses of power. I offer the concept of ephemeral permanence to express an impulse that, like an architect designing a building to sustain life, acknowledges that structures are inherently susceptible to the forces of human agency and time.

Republican design has continuously centered on these dual impulses—inhabitation and ephemeral permanence—taking up the task of instituting a political architecture capable of channeling human impulses, weaknesses, and proclivities into outlets that sustain, rather than undermine, the overarching structure of the political regime. James Madison's famous prescription, "Ambition must be made to counteract ambition," synthesizes these poles of inhabitation and ephemeral permanence (2003, p. 319). As a careful student of political history, Madison understood the risks of a system devoid of distinct channels for the expression—and controlled output—of energies that could prove fatal to its foundation. He recognized that to create an enduring system over time, albeit not indefinitely, a methodology of constitutional engineering that metabolized and regulated the adversarial forces and vices of human nature was required. For Madison, the challenge demanded a plan to remedy the systemic conditions that plague all republics: an unavoidable acceptance of demise (condition one: institutional inevitability) and the deployment of mechanisms (condition two: procedural contingency) to delay total collapse.

The Condition of Institutional Inevitability Spans the Corpus of Republican History Institutional inevitability denotes the republican acquiescence that decay is unavoidable—that all regimes eventually wither under the pressures of time, corruption, and mortality. We can locate this premise in Polybius's theory of governmental degeneration (*anacyclosis*), extending to Cicero and culminating in Rousseau, who likened the decline of a republic to the inevitable aging of the human body (Polybius in Pocock, 2003; Cicero, 2014; Rousseau, 1986a, 1986b). Maintenance of republican institutions is equivalent to the role of a physician who prescribes antidotes to mitigate the hardships of old age—alleviating symptoms while accepting the fact that death remains unavoidable. In *The Machiavellian Moment* (2003), J.G.A. Pocock examines Machiavelli's influence within the Savonarolan tradition, particularly the finite nature of republics. Pocock underscores the paradox inherent in republican structures: their vitality and eventual demise are intrinsically tied to their temporal and spatial contexts, with virtue as the central—yet fleeting—animating force (184–85).

This fatalistic view of political temporality, which finds roots in classical republican and early Christian traditions, further deepens the logic of institutional inevitability by framing decline as historical and theological—woven into the moral and metaphysical condition of human existence. This can be seen in the republican tradition, which incorporates a deterministic, quasi-Christian eschatological reading of history for the lifespan of a republic. Embedded within the architecture of the republic is an acknowledgment of its social constructiveness and, therefore, its ultimate impermanence. Just as humans are bound to birth, life, and death, so, too, are earthly political structures. In this view, questions of immortality or perpetuity are erased, particularly within an Augustinian reading of history. For Augustine, the distinction between the heavenly city (City of God) and the earthly city (City of Man) depicted human political structures as inherently corruptible, susceptible, and doomed by man's sinful nature (2003, Books XI–XIV). The earthly, human-made

City of Man was destined to decay and perish as the fallenness of its creators shaped its foundations (2003, Books XIX–XXII).

Post-Augustinian republican theory absorbed this fatalistic view of human nature, embedding the inevitability of decay into its understanding of political systems. The fallibility of man—carried by the mark of original sin—prefigures the lifespan of human structures of power and agency, tying their destiny to a *telos* of inescapable demise. Republican theorists and Christian theologians contemplated the same inevitability: the fall of man avows the belief that it is not a question of *if* but rather *when* the collapse of human political structures will happen. The central concern for republican theorists, as for Christian theologians, is the myopic realization of human ideals and survival marked by an omnipresent anticipation of destruction.

Both perspectives recognize that the structures they construct, no matter how meticulously calibrated, carry the seeds of their ruin within them. The republican project is constrained by this eschatological tension, situating its well-calibrated systems within historical processes bound to a terminal endpoint. The task, then, is not to prevent the fall but to *delay it*, to prolong the lifespan of the polity while at the same time addressing the certainty of its eventual demise. In this way, republican theory becomes a balancing act: a system design project that embraces human frailty while seeking to sustain the regime for as long as possible in the face of inescapable decline.

While Institutional Inevitability Lies at the Heart of the Republican Register, an Adjacent Concern Is Equally Foundational The second condition, procedural contingency, acknowledges the mortality of the republic—an affirmation of the first condition—as well as the mortality of those entrusted with safeguarding and sustaining the regime. Procedural contingency, by contrast, names the mechanisms—constitutional design, separation of powers, civic virtue—implemented to delay or regulate decline. This comprehensive framework encompasses various forms of political representation, from legislators to judges to noble courts. It also stresses an inventory of active civic responsibilities vested in a republican citizenry, crucial in maintaining social functionality and vitality. In this context, political agents refer to official representatives and a virtuous body of active citizens interconnected through a network of "relationships, procedures, politics, and social relations" (Benarieh Ruffer, 2013, p. 233). However, all categories of political actors are inevitably subject to the deteriorating effects of age, time, political capital, and health. Thus, a republican system of governance strives to ensure that the death of a singular leader—whether literal or electoral—or of a significant number of its members does not beget further death. Instead, it intends to fortify governing structures from sliding into a transition of particular loss to universal demise.

Inoculation against the contagion of death is imperative to prevent it from overwhelming the present moment's life force and disrupting the republic's structural foundations by compromising its operational capacities. To ensure stability and continuity, republican theory institutionalizes the condition of procedural contingency to assuage the impact and scope of death. This institutional response includes implementing clear lines of succession to ensure a seamless transfer of authority to safeguard against the destabilizing effects of mortality.

Succession Planning Occupied a Central Place in the Thinking of Ancient Philosophers In *Politics*, Aristotle (1981) emphasized the necessity of a transparent succession process as both a safeguard against arbitrary rule and a means of ensuring that decision-making mechanisms remained within the legal framework of the polity. For Aristotle, succession planning aligned with his broader objective: establishing a form of government grounded in institutional depth through a careful balance of power. Notably, he differentiated between regimes based on the number of rulers and whether they served self-interest or the common good. In doing so, he identified three ideal forms of rule—monarchy, aristocracy, and polity—alongside their corrupt counterparts: tyranny, oligarchy, and democracy. Central to this typology was the inevitability of decay, as internal and external pressures threatened the dissolution of form and the abandonment of the common good.

To counteract this tendency and ensure the stability and continuity of governance, Aristotle advocated for a mixed polity, blending elements of democracy and oligarchy. He believed such a hybrid system offered the greatest potential to render justice, balancing the interests of competing factions while tempering the extremes of the masses and the elite. Critically, Aristotle's regime classification underscores the condition of institutional inevitability and the necessity for governments to fortify their structures against decay proactively.

Similarly, Cicero, striving to cultivate stability, expressed deep trepidation about disruptions to *concordia*—a society's harmony. He argued that aligning mutual interests and fostering reciprocity among social classes could prevent the cleavages and factional divisions threatening the republic's stability. For Cicero, political leaders played a crucial role in maintaining this harmony. Symbolically, they served as a synthesis between the collective good and individual factional interests, acting as a stabilizing force within society. In Cicero's view, leadership was not a passive role but an active one—tasked with carefully balancing competing interests.

Fides, or trust—in both leaders and institutional arrangements—was equally central to Cicero's vision. He warned that the death of a political leader could weaken public trust, disrupt the daily functioning of the regime, and create instability. Such disruptions, he reasoned, could open dangerous fissures within the republic, leaving it vulnerable to exploitation and corruption (Cicero, 2014). Maintaining public trust in succession plans was thus critical, as the breakdown of *fides* often led to social discord and unrest.

Polybius, too, recognized the importance of well-defined succession plans within Rome's mixed constitution. He underscored their role in facilitating smooth transitions of power during crises, highlighting Rome's institutional flexibility—particularly its formal authorization of temporary emergency dictatorial powers. For Polybius, this adaptability legitimized "political conflict" without undermining public trust, enabling Rome to endure periods of strain (Wolin, 2004, p. 76).

However, Polybius shared the broader pessimism of Aristotle and Cicero, affirming the inevitability of decline known as *anacyclosis*—the natural regression of political regimes (Pocock, 2003, p. 70). In this cyclical model, monarchy devolves into tyranny, aristocracy into oligarchy, and democracy into *ochlos*, or mob rule. While Polybius acknowledged that degeneration was natural and inevitable, he believed the process could be delayed through mechanisms designed to foster institutional resilience. Rome's mixed constitution, he claimed, demonstrated this potential, offering enduring lessons in stable governance.

For Polybius, delaying *anacyclosis* required specific measures: fostering civic education to cultivate virtue and unity, harmonizing power among governmental departments, and ensuring the adaptability of governing institutions to address critical challenges quickly. While these measures could not permanently prevent decline, they could impede its effects—buying valuable time for the regime to stabilize itself.

Aristotle, Cicero, and Polybius accentuate the centrality of succession planning and institutional flexibility to regime survival. Their shared recognition of the inevitability of decay did not lead to resignation but to a focus on proactive measures—promoting trust, fostering harmony, and designing adaptable institutions to fortify governmental systems against their inherent vulnerabilities.

Later, Republican Thinkers and Projects Took up the Significance of Succession Planning, Recognizing It as Necessary for Producing Stability and Maintaining Continuity In Renaissance city-states like Florence and Venice, succession plans ensured smooth transitions of power to address the persistent worries of ancient thinkers: power vacuums, the erosion of public trust, and the destabilizing chaos unleashed by political upheavals. In sixteenth century Florence, the Medici family, while judiciously upholding the façade of republican governance, drew upon the register of republican thought to secure the stability and longevity of their rule (Kent, 2000, pp. 123–125). For the Medicis, the consolidation and maintenance of power were not merely minor tasks but governing imperatives, achieved by utilizing strategies that wove their influence seamlessly into the city's cultural and political fabric.

Aware of the pitfalls of disruptions to political leadership, the Medicis entrenched their dominance across generations through strategic marriages and astute appointments, nurturing alliances with prominent families that fortified their reign. Yet, their strategies ran deeper. The Medicis embedded themselves within Florence's institutional structures, manipulating the operations of the Signoria to consolidate their grip on power. As Machiavelli critiques in his *History of Florence* (1988), their capacity to blend republican rhetoric with oligarchic control was their potent skill, reflecting Florence's underlying political contradictions.

Meanwhile, Venice's system for electing the Doge exemplified a deliberate effort to safeguard the integrity of its republican government and ensure stability. The electoral process, established in the thirteenth century, involved a complex series of votes by elite councils, beginning with a random draw of electors from the Great Council and culminating in multiple rounds of selection and approval by smaller committees (Lane, 1973, pp. 199–201). This intricate procedure was designed to reduce the risk of individual manipulation, factionalism, and corruption in selecting the city's highest leader (Romano, 2007, pp. 45–47).

2.2 Two Existential Conditions of the Republican Body Politic

Venice balanced the need for continuity with accountability mechanisms by deploying rigorous, structured decision-making processes. These measures ensured that the Doge's power was recognized as legitimate yet tamed, embodying the Venetian values of collective decision-making and preventing abuses of power. In important ways, the Venetian system highlighted the republican condition of procedural contingency by ensuring that power transitions did not destabilize the regime but reinforced institutional resilience (Muir, 1981, pp. 112–114).

Similarly, following England's Glorious Revolution of 1688, succession planning gained new connotations as the monarchy's role was codified within a constitutional framework. The Bill of Rights (1689) and the Act of Settlement (1701) established clear procedural contingencies to address potential crises, such as the death or removal of political representatives, while also curbing abuses of power (Schwoerer, 1981, pp. 33–40; Vallance, 2006, pp. 285–290). This codification reflected a broader shift toward limiting arbitrary rule and safeguarding governance through legal structures. In England's case, we can observe how the concern over procedural contingency transcends republican theory, extending into other configurations of political governance, including monarchy. Precise succession planning is arguably even more vital to the legitimacy of a monarchy, as it establishes a generational sequence of authority that projects stability into the future.

Particularly important is how the codified practices of succession planning in the English case represent a move away from absolutism in a decisive step toward republican ideals such as the rule of law, representative governance, and the division of power. This shift highlights a fundamental political truth: disruptions to lines of authority cause existential concerns and anxieties about the future vitality of a political community. By institutionalizing succession, England sought to assuage these anxieties, creating a framework that reinforced the durability of its governance structures while reflecting broader ideological transformations.

The concern over procedural contingency exists outside the political history of Europe, reflecting a pervasive challenge for political units. For example, during the Ottoman Empire's classical period, laws of fratricide were employed to prevent violent contestation over leadership succession, ensuring stability in the aftermath of a ruler's death (Imber, 2002, pp. 51–54). Similarly, during the reigns of various Chinese dynasties, the practice of designating heirs served as a strategy to avert civil wars and maintain dynastic continuity (Lewis, 2009, pp. 201–204). These cursory examples illustrate that succession planning is not a uniquely European phenomenon but an issue inherent to the very nature of political communities: *who is to rule now, and who in the future?*

For Ancient and Modern Republican Thinkers Alike, the Republic's Lifespan Was Inherently Precarious Thus, the emphasis on succession planning—the second foundational condition of republican theory—could not be neglected without risking catastrophic consequences. By institutionalizing succession processes within constitutional frameworks, republican systems sought to mitigate conflicts, upheavals, and even the inevitability of death itself, transforming historical vulnerabilities into mechanisms of stability. The genius of the republican model lies in its ability to craft institutions that turn adverse conditions into enduring sources of strength.

Philip Pettit underscores the Herculean challenge of maintaining republican governance and institutional architecture, emphasizing the importance of deploying "devices" that produce "resilient" institutions designed to withstand challenges and endure over time (Pettit, 1997, p. 210). Resilience and transmutation are, therefore, first-order principles of republican theory, reinterpreting Nietzsche's famous assertion that "what doesn't kill me makes me stronger," though here in the context of institutional design (1997, p. 6).

The rich history of republican resilience, augmented by careful design, civic virtue, and calibrated succession, once formed the bulwark against collapse. Yet, for the American republic, the very architecture that has sustained its lifespan is now fracturing. As institutional safeguards weaken, what emerges to fill the void is not renewal but a reactive political energy that exploits the fear of decay rather than repairs it—an energy often mislabeled as populism.

In agreement with Jacques Rancière (2020), I contend there is much to gain by viewing populism not as a political form but as an interpretation: a narrative that obscures the structural logic of authoritarian consolidation. The term functions ideologically, attributing the erosion of democratic and republican institutions to the supposed will of "the people," typically imagined as irrational, suffering masses yearning for exclusion, order, and strongmen. But, as Rancière points out, the rise of figures like Donald Trump, Jair Bolsonaro, and Viktor Orbán reflects not the revolt of the underprivileged but the strategic maneuvers of oligarchic power, including the billionaire class, tech-overlords, conservative social forces, and disciplinary institutions. Populism, then, becomes a scapegoat, a rhetorical device that conceals the role of the economic and political establishment in advancing authoritarian governance. From the vantage point of republican theory, this is not merely a distortion but a direct threat. Populism collapses the temporal and procedural spacing that sustains republican governance, replacing deliberative authority with the immediacy of spectacle, rage, and affect. It stresses immediacy over process and physicalness over rationality and, in doing so, corrodes the very logic of procedural contingency that makes republics possible in the first place.

It is in this crisis of succession, fragility, and spiritual exhaustion that MAGA's apocalyptic promises take root. The figure of the necro-president does not arise in a vacuum; it is summoned within a condition that laments the present, mourns its future, and obsesses over its imminent demise. The necropolitical condition, accelerated by neoliberalization of all domains of life, the efficacy of nostalgic rhetoric, and systemic forms of institutional rot, makes the death drive of contemporary politics a pathological feature.

The emergence of the necro-president in the American republic signals this catastrophic inversion: a spectral figure of entropy presiding over institutions hollowed out by death. Here, governance is no longer driven by the vitality of life but by the machinery of decay. Death, once a force projected outward as a method of national preservation, now turns inward, delivering the spectacular horror of American carnage—not onto *them*, but on *us*. In this grotesque reversal, the republic confronts the ultimate collapse of its moral and structural foundations, awaiting its reckoning.

What I want to show next is how the necropolitical condition of the American republic transcends its theoretical framing and takes shape as a political technique. The procedural mechanisms once built to safeguard the republic—succession, legitimacy, public trust—are deteriorating. In their absence, what steps in to fill the void is not life but its uncanny double: a politics animated by death, spectacle, and symbolic resurrection.

References

Applebaum, A. (2020). *Twilight of democracy: The seductive lure of authoritarianism*. Knopf Doubleday Publishing Group.
Aristotle. (1981). *The Politics* (T. A. Sinclair, Trans.; T. J. Saunders, Rev.). Penguin Classics.
Augustine. (2003). *The city of god* (H. Bettenson, Trans.). Penguin Books.
Benarieh Ruffer, G. (2013). Legal modes and democratic citizens in republican theory. In A. Niederberger & P. Schink (Eds.), *Republican democracy* (pp. 229–247). Edinburgh University Press.
Breaugh, M., & Caivano, D. (2024). A living critique of domination: Exemplars of radical democracy from Black Lives Matter to #MeToo. *Philosophy & Social Criticism, 50*(3), 447–472.
Brown, W. (2015). *Undoing the demos: Neoliberalism's stealth revolution*. Zone Books.
Brown, W. (2019). *In the ruins of neoliberalism: The rise of antidemocratic politics in the West*. Columbia University Press.
Cicero, M. T. (2014). *On the republic and on the laws*. Cornell University Press.
Foucault, M. (2008). *The birth of biopolitics: Lectures at the Collège de France, 1978–79* (M. Senellart, Ed.; G. Burchell, Trans.). Palgrave Macmillan.
Imber, C. (2002). *The Ottoman Empire, 1300–1650: The structure of power*. Palgrave Macmillan.
Kent, D. V. (2000). *Cosimo de' Medici and the Florentine Renaissance: The patron's oeuvre*. Yale University Press.
Lane, F. C. (1973). *Venice: A maritime republic*. Johns Hopkins University Press.
Levitsky, S., & Ziblatt, D. (2018). *How democracies die*. Crown.
Lewis, M. E. (2009). *China's cosmopolitan empire: The Tang dynasty*. Harvard University Press.
Machiavelli, N. (1988). *History of Florence and of the affairs of Italy* (L. F. Banfield & H. C. Mansfield, Trans.). Princeton University Press.
Machiavelli, N. (1996). *Discourses on Livy* (H. C. Mansfield & N. Tarcov, Trans.). University of Chicago Press.
Machiavelli, N. (1998). *The Prince* (H. C. Mansfield, Trans.). University of Chicago Press.
Madison, J. (2003). Federalist no. 51. In A. Hamilton, J. Jay, & J. Madison (Eds.), *The federalist papers* (pp. 317–323). Signet Classics.
Montesquieu, C.-L. de S. (1973). *Persian letters* (C. J. Betts, Trans.). Penguin Books. (Original work published 1721).
Montesquieu, C.-L. de S. (2002). *The Spirit of the laws* (Translated and edited by A. M. Cohler, B. C. Miller, & H. S. Stone). Cambridge University Press. (Original work published 1748).
Mouffe, C. (2005a). *On the political*. Routledge.
Mouffe, C. (2005b). *The return of the political*. Verso.
Mouffe, C. (2013). Democratic citizenship and the political community. In J. Martin (Ed.), *Chantal Mouffe: Hegemony, radical democracy, and the political* (pp. 103–114). Routledge.

Mounk, Y. (2018). *The people vs. democracy: Why our freedom is in danger and how to save it.* Harvard University Press.

Muir, E. (1981). *Civic ritual in renaissance Venice.* Princeton University Press.

Näsström, S., & Kalm, S. (2015). A democratic critique of precarity. *Global Discourse, 5*(1), 23–38. https://doi.org/10.1080/23269995.2014.964604

Nietzsche, F. (1997). *Twilight of the idols* (R. Polt, Trans.). Hackett.

Pettit, P. (1997). *Republicanism: A theory of freedom and government.* Oxford University Press.

Pocock, J. G. A. (2003). *The Machiavellian moment: Florentine political thought and the Atlantic republican tradition.* Princeton University Press.

Rancière, J. (1999). *Disagreement: Politics and philosophy* (J. Rose, Trans.). University of Minnesota Press. (Original work published 1995).

Rancière, J. (2007). *Hatred of democracy* (S. Corcoran, Trans.). Verso. (Original work published 2005).

Rancière, J. (2020, February 24). *The crisis of democracy.* Verso Blog. https://www.versobooks.com/blogs/4576-jacques-ranciere-the-crisis-of-democracy

Romano, D. (2007). *The likeness of Venice: A life of Doge Francesco Foscari.* Yale University Press.

Rousseau, J.-J. (1986a). On the social contract. In F. Watkins (Ed.), *Political writings* (pp. 149–221). University of Wisconsin Press.

Rousseau, J.-J. (1986b). Constitutional project for Corsica. In F. Watkins (Ed.), *Political writings* (pp. 279–321). University of Wisconsin Press.

Schwoerer, L. G. (1981). *The declaration of rights, 1689.* Johns Hopkins University Press.

Snyder, T. (2017). *On tyranny: Twenty lessons from the twentieth century.* Penguin Books.

Vallance, E. (2006). *The glorious revolution: 1688—Britain's fight for liberty.* Abacus.

Vergara, C. (2021). Corruption as systemic political decay. *Philosophy and Social Criticism, 47*(3), 328–330.

Vergara, C. (2022). Republican constitutionalism: Plebian institutions and anti-oligarchic rules. *Theoria, 69*(2), 35–57.

West, C. (2005). *Democracy matters: Winning the fight against imperialism.* Penguin Books.

West, C. (2014). *Black prophetic fire.* Beacon Press.

Wolin, S. (2004). *Politics and vision: Continuity and innovation in Western political thought* (Expanded ed.). Princeton University Press.

Wolin, S. (2017). *Democracy incorporated: Managed democracy and the specter of inverted totalitarianism.* Princeton University Press.

Open Access This chapter is licensed under the terms of the Creative Commons Attribution 4.0 International License (http://creativecommons.org/licenses/by/4.0/), which permits use, sharing, adaptation, distribution and reproduction in any medium or format, as long as you give appropriate credit to the original author(s) and the source, provide a link to the Creative Commons license and indicate if changes were made.

The images or other third party material in this chapter are included in the chapter's Creative Commons license, unless indicated otherwise in a credit line to the material. If material is not included in the chapter's Creative Commons license and your intended use is not permitted by statutory regulation or exceeds the permitted use, you will need to obtain permission directly from the copyright holder.

Chapter 3
To Keep the Republic

A republic, if you can keep it.
Benjamin Franklin

Abstract I examine how the figure of the necro-president takes shape through three interrelated conditions of republican decline: constitutional anxiety around succession, the instrumentalization of death as a governing tool, and the collapse of procedural legitimacy, following the January 6, 2021, insurrection. These sites expose how the presidency has become a stage for symbolic decay, institutional fragility, and sovereign performance. In this chapter, I argue that the 2024 presidential campaign marked a new framing of Trump's messianic return—one that exceeded the restoration of law and instead emphasized resurrection as the condition for saving the republic. I explore how rhetoric, ritual, and spectacle were mobilized throughout the campaign to reclaim death as a source of vitality and to cast Trump as the only force capable of preventing the republic's final collapse.

Keywords Necro-president · Executive power · Presidential succession · Symbolic decay · Insurrection · Authoritarian revival · Institutional collapse

The necro-president haunts the scaffolding of governance. His emergence is not a rupture but a continuation—a spectral fulfillment of republican decay made flesh. The American presidency, long imagined as a seat of sovereign energy, is now defined by deterioration, doubt, and death. And yet, paradoxically, this very deathliness—this entropic vacuum—invites resurrection. Trump's return is not merely electoral; it is mythic. He reanimates the office through a violent promise: that he alone can reverse decay, banish weakness, and save the republic from its ghostly occupant. The necro-president becomes a symbol of decline and a political technique: death as spectacle, resurrection as governance. As Guy Debord (1994) suggests, the spectacle is not merely a visual display but a mode of governance in which appearance supplants substance and mediation replaces engagement. In this context, the presidency becomes a theater of death, where symbolic decay is commodified and exploited.

This chapter excavates the long-standing architectural anxiety embedded in republican design: what happens when the center cannot hold, and the figurehead becomes the symbol of decay? To unpack these anxieties, I engage with three interlocking dimensions of republican thought: the constitutional anxieties around succession and vitality; the executive as a death-wielding sovereign, positioned between messianic salvation and necropolitical control; and finally, the spectacle of death and procedural breakdown, culminating in the insurrection of January 6, 2021, and the 2024 election.

From these political dimensions—succession anxiety, sovereign death power, and spectacle—Trump emerges not only as a reaction *contra* decay but as its most skilled manipulator. He is the one who names death, channels its energy, and claims the mantle of survival. Entropy makes way for sovereignty as Biden's perceived decay becomes the condition for Trump's resurrection. Through spectacle and resurrectionist rhetoric, Trump positions himself as the ultimate necro-president of the *anti*-entropy force: not decaying but commanding death, not passive but sovereign. To understand how we arrived here, we must first turn to the architectural grammar of republican governance, where structure, succession, and decay have long haunted institutional designs.

Politics Is Architecture The enactment of politics in the public realm—what Hannah Arendt famously described as the "space of appearance" (1958, 1998)—is an architectural endeavor *par excellence*. Individuals and groups use language, symbols, and signs to ascribe meaning and construct figurative and physical communities. Cornelius Castoriadis (1997) identified this architectural dimension of politics, describing political systems as creations of collective imaginaries, products of deliberate design, contingency, and artificiality. Here, architecture serves as both metaphor and materiality: the design of republican institutions reflects and shapes the symbolic life of the political community. Viewing political action as an architectural expression highlights its performative dimensions, in a Butlerian sense, and its material foundations (Butler, 1988). The gathering of people, whether in consensus or conflict, transcends mere symbolism and embodies the corporeal nature of human existence in constructing an artifice for the playing out of politics embedded within nature. These architectural endeavors, marked by intimacy and disagreement, shape our physical and institutional structures.

Politics gives a name to contestations over foundational questions: where we should live, how we should live, who counts or belongs within the community, and how we ought to think and act on issues of collective importance. While the political process is never terminal, it creates life worlds, institutions, and structures imbued with the authority to govern, educate, control, and punish. In this light, politics is a sequential repetition of founding, destruction, and creation. Quentin Skinner (1984) and J.G.A. Pocock (1989, pp. 80–103) have demonstrated how, within the republican tradition, the act of founding establishes a republic's social, political, economic, and juridical domains. Historically, regime foundations have been justified by extra-social principles, such as divine right, tradition, and natural law, or by constructs grounded in popular sovereignty and the rule of law. Republican projects, in particular, emphasize popular sovereignty and the rule of law as the twin pillars of the political community. Founding, of course, is only the beginning; what follows is the challenge of succession and continuity.

3.1 Lines of Succession/Lines of Continuity

To partake in founding a republic is to set the boundaries for life within it, shaping what is possible through subsequent socio-cultural processes. No group of thinkers was more attuned to the dangers of ambiguous arrangements of power and authority—and the adverse effects they could produce—than the framers of the American republic. As Gordon Wood (1998, pp. 606–618) explains, the debates at the Constitutional Convention of 1787 over centralized versus decentralized governance, national security, and economic concerns shaped the design of the nascent political system. Central to these deliberations was the identification that unchecked actors and offices could invite corruption resulting in system destabilization. Thus, the architecture of the American republic was designed to provide both a stable foundation for governance and safeguards against poorly actualized agents of authority. These deliberations reflected deep anxieties about the fragility of leadership and the risks posed by disruptions to continuity.

Although succession planning surfaced primarily in the later stages of the convention—specifically about the vice presidency—the framers were acutely aware of the dangers posed by power vacuums (Pasley, 2016, p. 11). Their understanding of political history, informed by both ancient and the eighteenth century European precedents, underscored the importance of swift responses to potential vacancies in leadership. Despite the limited focus on this issue during the convention, the result was a detailed, albeit imperfectly narrow, succession plan embedded within the Constitution (Albert, 2011, p. 503). Article II, Section 1, Clause 6 stipulates that if a president's "removal, death, resignation, or inability to discharge the powers and duties of the office" occurs, the vice president shall assume the presidency (U.S. Constitution, 1787). This provision reflects a careful, pragmatic approach to procedural contingency, anticipating scenarios in which the stability of executive leadership might be threatened.

For the framers, disruptions to executive authority—whether due to internal challenges, external threats, or the inevitable fragility of human life—posed a serious risk to the republic's stability. Aware of his physical decline, Benjamin Franklin (1787) highlighted concerns about the capacity of elderly leaders to fulfill their duties, further underscoring the necessity of robust succession plans (Elkins &

McKitrick, 1993, pp. 529–540). These historical insights and practical considerations influenced the framers' design of the Constitution, embedding flexibility within the procedural framework for future revisions while addressing the immediate need for stability. The result was an architecture of governance that sought to balance ephemeral permanence with adaptability, ensuring the republic's endurance amid the uncertainties of social life.

In *Federalist No. 68*, Alexander Hamilton (2003, p. 412) defended the newly designed executive branch, emphasizing that the established electoral process would ensure smooth power transitions, provide institutional continuity, and prevent leadership vacuums. He argued that this process created a "moral certainty" against power struggles, showcasing a prime example of constitutional engineering. In *Federalist No. 70*, however, Hamilton shifted his focus, linking the vitality of the executive office to the physical and cognitive vigor of the individual occupying it. He insisted that an energetic, healthy, strong executive was indispensable to the stability of the federal government, warning that a "feeble executive" (2003, p. 422) would undermine it. Here, Hamilton's use of "feeble" referred not only to ineffective governance but also subtly to the physical and mental well-being of the president.

The framers' concerns about leadership and continuity in governance resonated in the rhetoric and institutional arrangements of the early republic. Centrally, there was an attentiveness that any person serving as a political representative—particularly as president—would inevitably confront the constraints of mortality. Envisioning a leader fit for such a high office requires a thorough consideration of the physical and mental fitness necessary to fulfill the responsibilities of the commander-in-chief.

With the widespread expectation that George Washington would become the first president following the ratification of the Constitution, concerns about the fitness of a person preparing for office became immediately relevant. At 57 years old, Washington was considered elder by the standards of the time, when life expectancy was significantly lower. Before taking office, Washington had survived several serious illnesses, including smallpox, malaria, and dysentery. These health challenges, combined with his age, heightened his awareness of the possibility of incapacitation or death while serving in office (Witt, 2001).

These concerns were not held exclusively by his supporters. Washington himself harbored doubts about his ability to endure the rigors of the presidency. In a private correspondence, he voiced apprehension about whether his health and stamina could sustain the demands of such an important role. Just weeks before his inauguration, Washington wrote to Major General Henry Knox, expressing profound reservations about assuming the presidency. He described his feelings as akin to a "culprit… going to the place of his execution" (Washington, 1789, pp. 2–3), capturing the heavy burden and anxiety he felt about the role. This analogy, though brief, signals the life-draining force of the office, hinting at the toll the presidency can exact on those who occupy it and the possibility of death within its domain. Later, in a June 15, 1790, letter to David Stuart, Washington detailed the health challenges he had faced during his first year in office, noting that he had been sicker in that year than in the preceding 30 years combined. He candidly acknowledged the likelihood of future illnesses and how they might inhibit his ability to effectively govern (Washington, 1790, pp. 523–528).

Washington's acute awareness of his health and the potential consequences of a vacant presidency motivated adopting further institutional safeguards to ensure the republic's continuity. Although the Constitution provided a basic succession plan, many perceived it as insufficient to fully guarantee stable leadership transitions. The ambiguity surrounding succession beyond the vice presidency—arguably a substantial shortcoming of the ratified Constitution—persisted after the Convention (Sindler, 1977).

The Presidential Succession Act of 1792 aimed to address this concern by establishing a line of succession, creating an institutional framework to mitigate the risks of a leadership vacuum. First, the act took for granted that the vice president would assume the presidency if the president could not fulfill their duties. Beyond this, Arthur Schlesinger (1974) documents the convoluted nature of the succession plan, writing, "If both the Presidency and the Vice Presidency were vacated, Madison's idea of an 'intermediate election' was to prevail. The President *pro tempore* of the Senate (or, if there were none, the Speaker of the House) would 'act as President … until a President be elected,' and a special election would be called for the next November to choose a new President unless the double vacancy occurred in the last months of the presidential term."

Concerns about the fitness of presidential candidates extended beyond physical health to encompass temperament, character, and ideology. In the 1796 presidential election, John Adams faced scathing criticism from his opponents, who characterized him as erratic and prone to fits of anger. These attacks suggested that his temperament rendered him unfit for office, undermining his capacity for effective governance (Elkins & McKitrick, 1993). Conversely, Adams's opponent, Thomas Jefferson, was criticized for his perceived radical ideas, which detractors argued posed a threat to the republic's stability (Pasley, 2016; Staloff, 2021). In this single election, we can find a spectrum of concerns stretching from comportment to ideology, highlighting the multifaceted scrutiny faced by early presidential contenders.

The subsequent election of 1800 intensified these partisan divisions, culminating in a fiercely contested and vitriolic campaign between Adams and Jefferson. Despite the acrimony, the election concluded with a peaceful transfer of power, marking a significant moment in the young republic's history. In his inaugural address on March 4, 1801, Jefferson sought to heal the nation's wounds, stating, "Every difference of opinion is not a difference of principle." Socialite Margaret Bayard Smith (1906) marveled at the tranquility of this transition, noting, "The changes of administration, which in every government and in every age have most generally been epochs of confusion, villainy, and bloodshed, in this our happy country take place without any species of distraction, or disorder."

Later, Jefferson himself reflected on the challenges of aging and its implications on public service. In a letter to John Adams in August 1816, Jefferson candidly divulges the decline of his physical and mental faculties with age and how it could hinder the present generation (1816, pp. 284–286). This moment of self-awareness revealed Jefferson's recognition of the precarious balance between individual vitality and the demands of public office.

The fragility of the presidency reached a critical juncture with the election of William Henry Harrison in 1840. At 68, Harrison was the oldest presidential candidate in US history at the time, sparking significant concerns about his ability to endure the pressures of the office. While the Whig Party framed Harrison as a rugged war hero and symbol of frontier resilience—epitomized in the campaign slogan "Tippecanoe and Tyler, Too"—his Democratic opponents pointed to his advanced age as a liability.[1] These concerns were tragically validated when Harrison died just 31 days into his term, marking the shortest tenure and the first death in office (Skaggs, 2014, p. xi).

Harrison's death in 1841 created a looming constitutional crisis, as the process for presidential succession had not yet been clearly defined. Vice President John Tyler assumed the presidency, setting an important precedent for full presidential succession, though this practice would not be codified until much later. Harrison's brief tenure and sudden death amplified anxieties about the office's vulnerabilities and underscored the necessity for precise succession mechanisms (Cash, 2018).

Concerns about an institutional power void persisted long after Harrison's death-inflicted presidency. Legislative efforts to clarify and strengthen the line of succession continued with the passage of the Presidential Succession Act of 1886, its revision in 1947, and its most recent amendment in 2006, which added the Secretary of Homeland Security to the order of succession. Today, the presidential line of succession includes 18 positions, beginning with the vice president and concluding with the Secretary of Homeland Security.[2] The depth of this succession line reflects an array of anxieties concerning the specter of a republic devoid of a figurehead and the uncertainty it engenders. These measures underscore a persistent acknowledgment of the fragile nature of leadership and the critical need for institutional safeguards to maintain stability in the face of mortality and unpredictable crises.

New provisions for succession planning also evolved within the Constitutional framework. The 25th Amendment, ratified in 1967, addressed the need to fill the vice president's office if it became vacant and allowed for the temporary transfer of

---

[1] For a complementary framing of Harrison as a war hero and champion of the frontier, see Ronald Shafer, *The Carnival Campaign: How the Rollicking 1840 Campaign of "Tippecanoe and Tyler Too" Changed Presidential Elections Forever* (Chicago: University of Chicago Press, 2016). Conversely, Harrison's critics did not refrain from depicting him as an out-of-touch drinking fiend; see Richard Carwardine, "Evangelicals, Whigs and the Election of William Henry Harrison," *Journal of American Studies* 17, no. 1 (1983): 61–76.

[2] For detailed accounts of these changes, see James E. Fleming, "Presidential Succession: The Art of the Possible," *Fordham Law Review* 79 (2010): 951–958; David A. Erhart, "I Am in Control Here: Constitutional and Practical Questions Regarding Presidential Succession," *University of Louisville Law Review* 51 (2012): 323–351; Arian Rubio, "Next in Line: Addressing the Constitutional & Policy Problems with the Current Presidential Line of Succession," *University of Michigan Journal of Law Reform* 58 (forthcoming, 2024); Roy E. Brownell, "The Executive Branch's Longstanding Embrace of Legislative Succession to the Presidency," *University of Memphis Law Review* 52 (2021): 281–420.

power from the president to the vice president. Providing much-needed clarity, the amendment outlines the succession process, including provisions for temporary transfers of power. This process was informally utilized in 1985 when President Reagan underwent surgery and formally invoked twice during George W. Bush's administration for medical procedures. The amendment also establishes a legal method for invoking an involuntary transfer of power in cases of presidential incapacity (Trautman, 2019, p. 393).

The meticulous—yet contested—process of establishing and recalibrating a succession plan reflects the institutional capacity of the American republic. It reinforces foundational principles of the Madisonian system: the careful delineation of governmental powers, the proper allocation of authority within legitimate channels, the harnessing of ambition within structured departments, and the division of power across federal and state governments. Such attention to ensuring stable and continuous power transfers generates legitimacy for the political system.

3.2 The Instrumentalization of Death

From its inception, the framers designed the executive office to project strength and authority—a concentrated embodiment of power and authority. As Hamilton emphasized, the president must avoid any hint of "feebleness," representing the collective vigor and determination of the American people. From George Washington to Donald Trump, the presidency has not merely served as a political office but as the ultimate personification of national identity and sovereignty. Presidential rhetoric and policies have steered the nation's trajectory, shaping its moral compass, economic direction, and military imperatives.

While the framers harbored concerns about the president accumulating excessive power, potentially resembling the unchecked bounds of a monarch, the reality that emerged in the centuries that followed was, in many ways, more disconcerting. Where the monarchical figurehead might claim divine right as God's servant on earth, the American president came to represent the complete, unfettered might of the state—what Hobbes termed the Leviathan, a "mortal god" tasked with preserving order and unity. Over time, this image evolved into what we now recognize as the unitary executive or the imperial presidency. Here lies the paradox: the virtues of strength and decisiveness essential to the presidency have also granted it the capacity to operate beyond the constraints of law, acting as both a paternalistic protector and a source of countless edicts of violence.

This duality is central to the American presidency finding its roots in constitutional design. For instance, the president's role as commander-in-chief extends far beyond military strategy. It grants the executive the ultimate power to arbitrate life and death—a power that, when magnified, takes on almost mythic proportions. The president becomes a beacon of hope, leading the nation like Moses, guiding his people out of the wilderness, and the agent of judgment, wielding the decree of death with the precision of the Angel of Death. This juxtaposition underscores the presidency's horrific grandeur: a life-giving force on the one hand and a harbinger of destruction on the other.

Nowhere is this more apparent than in the president's control over the instruments of state violence. As the head of the armed forces and the principal architect of foreign policy, the president can determine whose lives are deemed valuable and expendable. Whether in the form of nuclear or drone strikes or decisions to deploy troops, the presidency's exercise of power carries with it the weight of mortality. The president, in essence, becomes a sovereign figure capable of mediating life itself, deciding who shall live and who shall perish under the scorching heat of a thousand suns. President Harry S. Truman reflects on this exclusive power held by the president, stating, "And he alone, in all the world, must say Yes or No to that awesome, ultimate question: 'Shall we drop the bomb on a living target?'" (National Park Service, n.d.)

This returns us to an inescapable intersection between the two foundational conditions of republican governance: institutional inevitability and procedural contingency. While distinct, these conditions *overlap* in managing the president's adjudication over life and death. Historically, regimes have wielded the power of death as a deliberate strategy of self-preservation, enacted against perceived fears, real or imagined, internally and externally. In this process, death is not merely inevitable but instrumentalized—a state-sanctioned mechanism to regulate bodies, suppress dissent, and eliminate perceived threats to ensure the stability of the republic. This logic of cyclical violence justifies a range of actions, from public executions to mass incarceration to warfare, all framed as necessary to stave off institutional decay. Death is thus imbued with the juridical order legitimized as a force for preserving domestic and international order. This approach reveals the republic's *modus operandi*: its stability is maintained by rendering specific populations disposable, framing their exclusion and elimination as necessary to preserve national security and progress.

This leads us naturally to the work of scholars who have explored the deeper mechanics of how regimes regulate the boundaries between life and death. Michel Foucault, Giorgio Agamben, and Achille Mbembe have demonstrated how systems of governance embed the management of mortality into their institutional frameworks, placing death simultaneously inside and outside of the juridical order. Foucault's concept of biopower (2003) offers a lens to understand how modern governance prioritizes regulating life while systematically wielding death as a method of control. This interplay is not incidental but central to the logic of governmentality, where the state's influence permeates nearly every sphere of social existence—extending its reach from health care and law enforcement to food and drug regulation.

The logic of biopower is inscribed in the history, structure, and policies of mass incarceration. At its core, the prison system is built on the principle of creating physical structures to conduct the systematic disappearance of human lives. As Angela Davis (1998) argues, prisons achieve a "feat of magic" by creating the illusion that social problems are resolved while erasing the individuals and communities most affected by those problems. The proliferation of the prison-industrial complex, which profits from and normalizes governmental and corporate control over historically racialized and economically and politically disenfranchised populations, cloaks its lethal justifications behind the façade of public safety.

The sprawling network of prisons and jails across the United States exemplifies the instrumentalization of death by the American state. This machinery of governance transforms caging humans, exploiting surplus labor power, and even state-sanctioned execution into functional tools of institutional self-preservation. The American prison system encapsulates the contradictions of the republic, exposing the state's inherent history of violence in its metastasizing presence even as the foundations of the republic tremble under the weight of its decay.

Agamben's work (1998, 2005) explores how regimes can reduce individuals to "bare life"—a purely biological existence devoid of social and political rights. Those reduced to bare life are placed in a "state of exception," a concept Agamben traces back to ancient Roman law, which permits a regime to decide who "may be killed and yet not sacrificed" (Agamben, 1998, p. 12) as part of its regulation of life and death. In the context of the global War on Terror, American foreign and domestic policy sought to address the condition of institutional inevitability. Actions such as ground invasions, domestic spying and wiretapping, enhanced interrogations, and indefinite detentions at Guantanamo Bay—widely condemned by the international community as violations of international law and norms—were framed as necessary preventive measures. Aligned with Agamben's analysis, American policy not only determined who "may be killed and yet not sacrificed" but also justified the implementation of "shock and awe" tactics to deploy death as a means of saving the republic from the devastation unleashed by the 9/11 attacks.

Agamben's identification of the "state of exception" and its manifestation in American policies during the War on Terror parallels the broader strategy of regimes that instrumentalize death to preserve institutional stability. The War on Terror, much like the prison-industrial complex, reveals how the American state employs biopolitical techniques to delineate which lives are deemed expendable and which are worth preserving. The indefinite detentions at Guantanamo Bay, which, as of early 2025, sits at nine detainees, continue to serve as a modern form of systemic disappearance, maintaining control through extrajudicial detention (The New York Times, 2024). This practice became further entrenched during the early weeks of the second Trump administration, which expanded the prison's role to serve as a detention site for migrants.

In March 2025, Venezuelan nationals residing in the United States—deemed illegal and accused of affiliation with the transitional crime organization Tren de Aragua—were apprehended and flown to a maximum-security prison in El Salvador. Despite a temporary restraining order issued by US District Judge James Boasberg blocking these deportations, the administration proceeded with the flights under the legal justification of the 1798 Alien Enemies Act, leading to significant legal and constitutional disputes (J.G.G. v. Trump, 2025). These developments threaten to erode further legal protections for migrants and refugees, as well as suggest an expansion of the use of indefinite detention for both national security and immigration control purposes.

Mbembe's concept of necropolitics (2001, 2003) shows how states extend their control by deploying a matrix of violence that transcends traditional mechanisms of punishment through the determination of who may live and who must die. This framework creates a pervasive sense of omnipresent, imminent death within the state, coupled with reactionary preventive deterrence as a core function of state power. The regulation of death, as described by Mbembe, becomes entangled in cyclical patterns of violence—preventive, reactionary, and rehabilitative—that repeat endlessly. The self-perpetuating and self-justifying nature of state-sanctioned violence is framed within discourses of necessity, positioning such measures as essential bulwarks against institutional decay, collapse, and eventual death. Mbembe's insights into the cyclical nature of state-sanctioned violence show how institutional decay is staved off through the perpetual enactment of death—whether via the targeted disappearances imposed by mass incarceration, the extrajudicial killings justified under the War on Terror, or the pervasive police violence against Black men. These practices exemplify how death is operationalized and instrumentalized to maintain state authority and preserve institutional stability.

Foucault, Agamben, and Mbembe provide critical insights into how states deploy technological, ideological, and discursive tools to regulate bodies. This regulation—from medical to juridical spaces—shapes individuals into subjected beings, rendering some lives valuable to social utility while deeming others expendable. Their analyses reveal that control extends beyond behavioral regulation to determining life and death. Whether justified through security, racial purity, or resource scarcity, regulating bodies inherently carry the possibility of termination. This power to govern life prefigures a kind of inverted agency—one not grounded in preservation but in a form of systemic suicide.

Historically and in the present, the American republic has institutionalized death as a mechanism of self-preservation, extending its deterministic trajectory of decay. From the genocidal occupation and dispossession of Indigenous lands to the racial violence of chattel slavery and the modern prison-industrial complex, the republic has operated as an agent of death, targeting dehumanized populations. Systems of coloniality, racism, classism, ableism, and other forms of oppression underpin this violence, framing it as a necessary safeguard against collapse. By examining the structural inevitability of this violence, a macabre history emerges—one in which the republic's survival has been secured through the systemic normalization of the administration of death.

This underscores how the cyclical regulation of life and death is intrinsic to republican theory. More specifically, it reveals how this logic—embedded within legal and moral frameworks—elevates institutional preservation above human life. In this schema, individuals are rendered expendable, reduced to mere instruments serving the state's continuity.

Yet, the nature of this regulatory power extends beyond the transactional; it is ontological. The ability to determine who lives and who dies presupposes a decision enacted by living actors operating within governing structures. But what happens when these actors—the executioner, the slaveholder, the drone pilot—are perceived as lifeless? When death is no longer an external force to be imposed but an internalized condition of social life, the actors and institutions tasked with sustaining order become obsolete.

In this context, Jabbar's truck rampage in New Orleans and Livelsberger's suicidal explosion in Las Vegas become legible only within a framework of mutilated bodies, torched steel, and shattered glass. In this society, death is systematically administered and weaponized. The political aphorism "my body, my choice" offers a false promise, concealing the illusion of sovereignty in the face of external control. Yet, the specter of death permeates these structures, embodying both the inevitability of natural decay and the calculated interventions of those who wield death as an instrument of governance. These forces rationalize collective rituals of mourning, remembrance, and even celebration. A constellation reading of Foucault, Agamben, and Mbembe reveals this veiled logic of governance, where life and death are perpetually entangled.

However, Trump is not simply a continuation of this death logic but a culmination of it. He reframes death not as an inevitability to be staved off but as a governing tool to be wielded with theatrical panache. His rallies become ritual performances of resurrection, where the symbols of decay—crime, borders, Democrats—are named and exorcised. His body becomes the anti-entropy machine: defiant, unaging, vigorous, untouchable. And crucially, during the 2024 campaign, Trump framed Biden as a figure of entropy: senile, disoriented, barely alive. In doing so, Trump casts himself not merely as a necro-sovereign but as the only force capable of halting the republic's terminal drift.

Through Christian media and conspiratorial iconography—including Jesus appearing in courtroom sketches, videos proclaiming "God made Trump," and recurrent comparisons to Cyrus the Great—Trump is coded as a messianic figure, divinely tasked with staving off collapse. As Layne and Slattery (2024) report, evangelical outlets increasingly claim Trump as a modern-day Cyrus, the pagan liberator who restored God's order. A 2024 campaign video, shared widely on social media, begins with the narration: "God looked down on his planned Paradise and said, I need a caretaker. So God gave us Trump" (NPR, 2024). This fusion of providence and personality cult is further dramatized in a viral image, circulated online and endorsed by Trump himself, that places a spectral Jesus standing behind him in court. As Margaret Hartmann (2023) observes, although the sketch was neither official nor particularly convincing, it was embraced by his followers as "the most accurate court sketch of all time." In this eschatological imaginary, God didn't just make Trump—He sent him to redeem the republic from decay.

In this reading, Trump is not death incarnate. He is anti-death. He is the sovereign who names the dying, purges the weak, and promises national resurrection. While Biden governs over decay, Trump performs vitality. While Biden is entropy, Trump is the last gasp of form—authoritarian, theatrical, mythic. The presidency under Trump becomes a sacrificial ritual, a stage for demonstrating who must die for the republic to live. And Trump—branded, anointed, resurrected—is the high priest of that sacrifice.

The emergence of the necro-president in the American republic signals a catastrophic reversal: a spectral figure presiding over institutions hollowed out by death. Governance is no longer animated by vitality but driven by the machinery of decay. Death, once projected outward, now turns inward—delivering the *spectacular horror of American carnage not to them but to us*.

In this grotesque exchange, the republic confronts the ultimate collapse of its moral and structural foundations, suspended in anticipation of its reckoning. If succession planning reveals the republic's anxiety about mortality, and the presidency's symbolic role includes mediating death, what happens when those procedures become hollowed out?

3.3 The Subversion of Procedural Contingency

The deficiencies of the American political system are often downplayed through comparisons with other systems in a global context. By framing America's institutional and cultural flaws as relatively minor or less significant than those of other nations, historians, political scientists, and policymakers have perpetuated the narrative of American exceptionalism. This narrative relies on quantitative categories to support a central thesis of superiority. Analyses frequently frame the American republic as a paradigm of stability, citing indices such as freedom of the press, social mobility, a lack of political or religious persecution, and high living standards. Central to this depiction of the American political system as healthy, stable, and flourishing is the idea that the rule of law remains the foundational basis of the republic.

The structural integrity of this foundation is tested every four years during the transfer of presidential power. Commentators often emphasize that, unlike in other nations, the machinery of governance and decision-making—along with the power vested in the executive branch—is never jeopardized during these transitions.[3] Even during brief intervals when a political office is vacant, as one administration ends and another begins, these *gaps* are portrayed as non-perilous. The peaceful transfer of power implicitly lies at the heart of arguments professing the health and greatness of the American political system.

However, the January 6, 2021, insurrection directly complicates this interpretation of stability and resilience. Historically, institutional mechanisms had ensured smooth transitions of power, even during national crises such as assassinations (Lincoln, Garfield, McKinley, Kennedy), natural deaths in office (Harrison, Taylor, Harding, Roosevelt), or contentious elections (Jefferson, J.Q. Adams, Hayes,

---

[3] For brief examples, see *The Economist*, "Orderly Transfers of Power Occur Less Often Than You Might Think," October 16, 2020, https://www.economist.com/graphic-detail/2020/10/16/orderly-transfers-of-power-occur-less-often-than-you-might-think; and Partnership for Public Service, 2023 *Presidential Transition Guide* https://presidentialtransition.org/wp-content/uploads/sites/6/2023/11/2023-Presidential-Transition-Guide.pdf

3.3 The Subversion of Procedural Contingency

G.W. Bush). Yet, Trump's contestation of the 2020 election results and the attack at the US Capitol dislodged this historical reality. While the events of that day have been extensively documented, the characterization of activity remains fiercely debated. Some view January 6 as a violent mob riot, others as an attempted coup or insurrection, and still others as a patriotic demonstration akin to the spirit of 1776 (Anker, 2023). Regardless of these differing interpretations, one point is clear: Donald Trump was the centrifugal force whose rhetoric and actions ignited the event.

It was Trump who, in an incendiary speech, urged his supporters to "fight like hell" (BBC News, 2021). It was Trump who pressured then-Vice President Mike Pence to suspend the certification of the Electoral College results. It was Trump's supporters who chanted, "Hang Mike Pence!" (Swan & Cheney, 2022), breached the US Capitol, vandalized property, and mocked the legislative process. Unreflectively propagating the hegemonic narrative of America's exceptional political system, the former vice president recounts the scene of January 6: "To see fellow Americans ransacking the Capitol left me with a simmering indignation and the thought: Not here, not this… *not in America*" (Pence, 2022, p. 3; emphasis original). The violence resulted in five deaths during the attack, including a Capitol Police officer, as well as the subsequent suicides of four other officers. In an ironic twist, Trump's invocation of fighting would later become a rallying cry for his 2024 presidential campaign, offered in the frantic moments following an ill-fated alleged assassination attempt against him.

First as Tragedy, Then as Farce January 6 continues to resonate in the American political consciousness—not merely as a moment of chaos but as a profound revelation of the system's fragility. The day laid bare how few actors are needed to disrupt constitutional processes and circumvent the rule of law. It exposed a critical pressure point within the republic: the vulnerability of leadership continuity and the transfer of power. Ultimately, it revealed the precariousness of the American republic's foundations, echoing the founders' concerns nearly 250 years ago. Interruptions in leadership and fissures in authority, as the founders feared, have the potential to render the republic groundless.

Francis Fukuyama and other scholars have diagnosed the American republic as a decaying system marked by "dysfunctional" governing institutions. In this light, January 6 is a stark illustration of this decline. The legitimacy and stability of the presidency—once envisioned as a stabilizing force—are now riddled with fractures, threatening its ability to anchor the broader political order. The events of that day are not merely a reflection of Trump's influence but a symptom of deeper systemic decay, calling into question whether the republic's foundational principles can endure in an era of heightened fragility and dysfunction.[4]

---

[4] While I am hesitant to use the term "consensus," there is undeniably broad agreement on the decline of the American political system. Across ideological divides—conservatives and progressives, nationalists and radicals alike—many contend that the state of the American republic is in jeopardy. See Francis Fukuyama, "Rotten to the Core? How America's Political Decay Accelerated During the Trump Era," *Foreign Affairs* 18 (2021); Francis Fukuyama, *Political Order and Political*

The critical nature of January 6 brings us back to the underlying anxieties inherent in republican theory. When the transfer of power no longer confirms the stability of a juridical anchoring but becomes a site of contestation, the *subversion and deficiency of procedural contingency are exposed*. In the MAGA view, the ascension of Biden to the presidency nullified institutional mechanisms designed to produce continuous lines of authority. With the efficacy of procedural safeguards left tenuous, the fear of institutional inevitability superseded the mechanisms designed to preserve stability, exposing vulnerable cracks in the system.

During the 2024 presidential campaign, the failure of procedural contingency revealed on January 6—and the lingering allegations of election fraud from 2020—receded in prominence, overshadowed by an even graver concern: a growing belief among right-wing proponents that the republic faced an existential crisis. What began as a criticism of Biden's decision to stay in the race, citing his age and a disastrous June debate, morphed into a more ominous narrative. The president—and, by extension, the office—came to symbolize decay and death.

As this narrative deepened, MAGA discourse increasingly claimed that institutional safeguards had failed, confirming the symbolic rupture of January 6. The presidency was recast as an empty vessel: manipulated, hollow, and stripped of legitimacy. This shift reflects a longer arc in the Republican Party's trajectory since the late 1960s, characterized by a demand for a more assertive, centralized executive. As Jacobs and Milkis (2022, p. 224) observe, Trump embodies a "symptom of" executive-centered governance. They argue that Trump's appeal drew strength from a widespread perception that the nation was in decline, lacking leadership capable of restoring its former greatness. The electoral process, then, became not just a political mechanism but a ritual of redemption, vital to reversing the perceived decay of the republic.

Trump's 2016 victory over Hillary Clinton reinforced this belief for his supporters, signaling a reclaiming of greatness. In contrast, Biden's 2020 success—followed by persistent accusations of election theft—revived long-standing fears of Democratic corruption and catalyzed deeper anxiety: the country was drifting toward collapse. This sentiment soon hardened into an eschatological vision, framing the republic's survival as dependent on resurrecting a strong executive figure.

Although claims of electoral fraud were thoroughly debunked, Trump and his allies continued to propagate these falsehoods throughout the 2024 election cycle. After the failed Capitol insurrection and the rejection of numerous legal challenges, MAGA rhetoric mutated. What had begun as accusations of voter fraud expanded into broader claims of government tyranny. The "Stop the Steal" campaign evolved beyond its initial focus, embedding itself in the cultural and psychological fabric of far-right conservatism (Salek, 2023). The narrative now held a deep suspicion—not just of the election but of the legitimacy of the federal government itself.

Decay: From the Industrial Revolution to the Globalization of Democracy (New York: Farrar, Straus and Giroux, 2014b); Francis Fukuyama, "America in Decay: The Sources of Political Dysfunction," *Foreign Affairs* 93 (2014a); and Francis Fukuyama, "The Decay of American Political Institutions," *The American Interest* 9, no. 3 (2013): 6–19.

Biden's presidency became the central symbol of this distrust. His age and visible cognitive decline were interpreted as metaphors for institutional fragility, reviving classical republican anxieties about decay and disorder. He was portrayed not merely as an illegitimate leader but as the embodiment of rot—a necro-president whose presence accelerated the republic's collapse. This framing fused the image of an ailing mortal with the once-stabilizing institution of the presidency, recasting it as corrupted, volatile, and incapable of renewal.

In this chapter, I have sought to show the constitutional mechanics of death and the symbolic erosion that follows when those mechanisms no longer inspire trust, vitality, or continuity. In that void, the necro-president emerges—not as an aberration, but as the inevitable outcome of a republic that has forgotten how to regenerate.

Death Had Arrived for the Republic There can be no resurrection without a corpse. And in the theater of American decline, the presidency has become that corpse—ritualized, embalmed, endlessly mourned. Trump doesn't hide the decay; he puts it on display. He stages the collapse so he can perform the revival. And, in the end, the necro-president isn't a warning. He's the prophecy fulfilled. *Behold the man—Ecce homo. Behold the necro-president.*

References

Agamben, G. (1998). *Homo sacer: Sovereign power and bare life*. Stanford University Press.
Agamben, G. (2005). *State of exception*. University of Chicago Press.
Albert, R. (2011). The constitutional politics of presidential succession. *Hofstra Law Review, 39*(3), 497–576.
Anker, E. (2023). Ugly freedoms and the January 6 insurrection. In J. R. Di Leo & S. A. McClennen (Eds.), *Left theory and the alt-right*. Routledge.
Arendt, H. (1998). *The human condition*. University of Chicago Press. (Original work published 1958).
BBC News. (2021, February 13). Capitol riots: Did Trump's words at rally incite violence? *BBC News*. https://www.bbc.com/news/world-us-canada-55640437
Brownell, R. E. (2021). The executive branch's longstanding embrace of legislative succession to the presidency. *University of Memphis Law Review, 52*, 281–420.
Butler, J. (1988). Performative acts and gender constitution: An essay in phenomenology and feminist theory. *Theatre Journal, 40*(4), 519–531. http://www.jstor.org/stable/3207893
Carwardine, R. (1983). Evangelicals, Whigs and the election of William Henry Harrison. *Journal of American Studies, 17*(1), 47–75.
Cash, J. T. (2018). The principle of executive continuity: Constitutional crises and the reinterpretation of presidential power. *American Political Thought, 7*(1), 26–56.
Castoriadis, C. (1997). *The imaginary institution of society* (K. Blamey, Trans.). MIT Press.
Davis, A. (1998, September 10). Masked racism: Reflections on the prison industrial complex. *Colorlines*. https://www.colorlines.com/articles/masked-racism-reflections-prison-industrial-complex
Debord, G. (1994). *The Society of the Spectacle* (D. Nicholson-Smith, Trans.). Zone Books. (Original work published 1967).
Elkins, S. M., & McKitrick, E. (1993). *The age of federalism: The early American Republic, 1788–1800*. Oxford University Press.

Erhart, D. A. (2012). "I am in control here": Constitutional and practical questions regarding presidential succession. *University of Louisville Law Review, 51*, 323–351.

Fleming, J. E. (2010). Presidential succession: The art of the possible. *Fordham Law Review, 79*, 951–958.

Foucault, M. (2003). *"Society must be defended": Lectures at the Collège de France, 1975–1976* (D. Macey, Trans.). Picador.

Franklin, B. (1787). Statement at the Constitutional Convention, as recorded by James McHenry. In C. A. Beard (Ed.), *The enduring federalist* (pp. 42–43). Collier Books.

Fukuyama, F. (2013). The decay of American political institutions. *The American Interest, 9*(3), 6–19.

Fukuyama, F. (2014a). *Political order and political decay: From the industrial revolution to the globalization of democracy*. Farrar, Straus and Giroux.

Fukuyama, F. (2014b). America in decay: The sources of political dysfunction. *Foreign Affairs, 93*, 5.

Fukuyama, F. (2021). Rotten to the core? How America's political decay accelerated during the Trump era. *Foreign Affairs, 18*.

Hamilton, A. (2003). "Federalist no. 68" and "Federalist no. 70". In I. A. Hamilton, J. Madison, & J. Jay (Eds.), *The federalist papers* (pp. 412–422). Signet Classics.

Hartmann, M. (2023, October 6). Trump's Jesus court sketch is even worse than it looks. *New York Magazine*. https://nymag.com/intelligencer/2023/10/trumps-jesus-court-sketch-is-even-worse-than-it-looks.html

J.G.G. v. Trump (2025). No. 1:25-cv-00766 (D.D.C. filed Mar. 15, 2025). https://www.courtlistener.com/docket/69741724/jgg-vtrump/

Jacobs, N., & Milkis, S. M. (2022). Conservatism transformed: The Republican Party since 1960. In *What happened to the vital center? Presidentialism, populist revolt, and the fracturing of America*. Oxford University Press.

Jefferson, T. (1801, March 4). *First Inaugural Address*. Retrieved from https://www.loc.gov/exhibits/creating-the-united-states/inaugural-address.html

Jefferson, T. (1816). To John Adams, August 1. In J. J. Looney (Ed.), *The papers of Thomas Jefferson, retirement series, Vol. 10: May 1816 to 18 January 1817* (pp. 284–286). Princeton University Press.

Layne, N., & Slattery, G. (2024, March 22). 'God gave us Trump': Christian media, evangelicals preach messianic message. *Reuters*. https://www.reuters.com/world/us/god-gave-us-trump-christian-media-evangelicals-preach-messianic-message-2024-03-22/

Mbembe, A. (2001). *On the postcolony*. University of California Press.

Mbembe, A. (2003). Necropolitics. *Public Culture, 15*(1), 11–40. https://doi.org/10.1215/08992363-15-1-11

National Park Service. (n.d.). Truman and the atomic bomb. https://www.nps.gov/articles/trumanatomicbomb.htm

NPR. (2024, January 26). A video making the rounds online depicts Trump as a Messiah-like figure. *NPR Morning Edition*. https://www.npr.org/2024/01/26/1227070827/a-video-making-the-rounds-online-depicts-trump-as-a-messiah-like-figure

Partnership for Public Service. (2023, November). *2023 Presidential Transition Guide*. Partnership for Public Service. https://presidentialtransition.org/wp-content/uploads/sites/6/2023/11/2023-Presidential-Transition-Guide.pdf

Pasley, J. L. (2016). *The first presidential contest: 1796 and the founding of American Democracy*. University Press of Kansas.

Pence, M. (2022). *So help me god*. Simon & Schuster.

Pocock, J. G. A. (1989). *Politics, language and time: Essays on political thought and history*. University of Chicago Press.

Rubio, A. (2024). Next in line: Addressing the constitutional & policy problems with the current presidential line of succession. *University of Michigan Journal of Law Reform, 58*. (in press).

Salek, T. A. (2023). Deflecting deliberation through rhetorical nihilism: 'Stop the Steal' as an unethical and intransigent rival public. *Communication and Democracy, 57*(1), 94–118.

References

Schlesinger, A. M., Jr. (1974). On the presidential succession. *Political Science Quarterly, 89*(3), 475–505.

Shafer, R. (2016). *The carnival campaign: How the rollicking 1840 campaign of "Tippecanoe and Tyler Too" changed presidential elections forever*. Chicago Review Press.

Sindler, A. P. (1977). *Unchosen Presidents: The Vice-President and other frustrations of Presidential succession*. University of California Press.

Skaggs, D. C. (2014). *William Henry Harrison and the conquest of the Ohio country: Frontier military campaigns, 1784–1814*. Johns Hopkins University Press.

Skinner, Q. (1984). The idea of negative liberty: Philosophical and historical perspectives. In R. Rorty, J. B. Schneewind, & Q. Skinner (Eds.), *Philosophy in history* (pp. 193–224). Cambridge University Press.

Smith, M. B. (1906). In G. Hunt (Ed.), *The first forty years of Washington Society*. Charles Scribner's Sons.

Staloff, D. (2021). The philosophical politics of Jefferson and Adams. In D. Gish & A. Bibby (Eds.), *Rival visions: How Jefferson and his contemporaries defined the early American republic* (pp. 38–73). University of Virginia Press.

Swan, B. W., & Cheney, K. (2022, May 25). Trump expressed support for hanging Pence during Capitol riot, Jan. 6 testimony reveals. *Politico*. https://www.politico.com/news/2022/05/25/trump-expressed-support-hanging-pence-capitol-riot-jan-6-00035117

The Economist. (2020, October 16). Orderly transfers of power occur less often than you might think. *The Economist*. https://www.economist.com/graphic-detail/2020/10/16/orderly-transfers-of-power-occur-less-often-than-you-might-think

The New York Times. (2024, December 31). *The Guantánamo Docket*. https://www.nytimes.com/interactive/2021/us/guantanamo-bay-detainees.html

Trautman, L. J. (2019). The Twenty-Fifth Amendment: Incapacity and ability to discharge the powers and duties of office. *Cleveland State Law Review, 67*(3), 497–576.

U.S. Constitution. (1787). Article II, Section 1, Clause 6.

Washington, G. (1789). From George Washington to Henry Knox, 1 April 1789. In D. Twohig (Ed.), *The papers of George Washington, Presidential series, Vol. 2: 1 April 1789–15 June 1789* (pp. 2–3). University Press of Virginia.

Washington, G. (1790). From George Washington to David Stuart, 15 June 1790. In D. Twohig, M. A. Mastromarino, & J. D. Warren (Eds.), *The papers of George Washington, Presidential series, Vol. 5: 16 January 1790–30 June 1790* (pp. 523–528). University Press of Virginia.

Witt, C. B. (2001). The health and controversial death of George Washington. *Ear, Nose & Throat Journal, 80*(2), 102–105.

Wood, G. S. (1998). *The creation of the American Republic, 1776–1787*. University of North Carolina Press.

Open Access This chapter is licensed under the terms of the Creative Commons Attribution 4.0 International License (http://creativecommons.org/licenses/by/4.0/), which permits use, sharing, adaptation, distribution and reproduction in any medium or format, as long as you give appropriate credit to the original author(s) and the source, provide a link to the Creative Commons license and indicate if changes were made.

The images or other third party material in this chapter are included in the chapter's Creative Commons license, unless indicated otherwise in a credit line to the material. If material is not included in the chapter's Creative Commons license and your intended use is not permitted by statutory regulation or exceeds the permitted use, you will need to obtain permission directly from the copyright holder.

Chapter 4
The Necro-President

> *Sovereign is he who decides on the exception.*
> Carl Schmitt

Abstract In this chapter, I argue that the figure of the necro-president reaches its full articulation during the 2024 election cycle, where political spectacle, institutional decay, and symbolic death converge into a new logic of rule. I track how Biden's presidency became a site of projected mortality, and how Trump's campaign transformed death into a political resource, used not only to delegitimize opposition but to cast himself as a messianic figure capable of resurrecting the republic. I weave insights from Arendt, Han, Lefort, Benjamin, Derrida, and Anderson to frame death as a material force shaping contemporary governance. I argue that death becomes the mechanism through which authority is asserted, institutions are hollowed out, and legitimacy is claimed. The necro-president is not just a figure of decline. He is a structure of rule built through decay.

Keywords Necro-president · Executive power · Trumpism · Spectacle politics · Institutional collapse · Authoritarianism · Political messianism · Conspiracism

A republican form of government is ontologically anxious, animated by concerns, trepidations, and predictions of doom. Throughout the long tradition of republican thought, the temptation for structural immortality has been met with institutional responses to assuage these fears. As a result, the design of republican architecture is central to the task of conceiving, founding, sustaining, and expanding a regime. As I have shown, two pulsating, imminent concerns that seek to address this anxiety—institutional inevitability and procedural contingency—have shaped the contours of the republican tradition, particularly within the American republic.

Key to preserving and prolonging the republic's life has been instrumentalizing the very fear that animates it: death. Republican regimes have fortified their institutional structures by managing and regulating life and death. This function—the administration of death—was codified into the juridical order of the American republic *qua* Constitution, vesting this monolithic power in a specific seat of authority: the President of the United States. The president, serving as commander-in-chief, is not merely a military leader in the simplest sense but the ultimate source of adjudication over matters of life and death.

Our present political moment presents a profound dilemma. Allegations of societal decline are not unique to American society; however, what is distinct today is how this decline has been linked not strictly to moral perversion, political or economic corruption, or even a lack of civic virtue but to death itself. The ultimate fear of republican theory assumes an internalized existential confrontation grappling with the inescapable realization that everything, including the republic itself, dies.

4.1 "Proof of Life"

The 2024 presidential election denotes a momentous point where anxieties of collapse and death reach their zenith. It symbolizes the arrival of the republic's death incarnate in the figure of the necro-president. Such proximity to death—embodied in the president—recalls, to borrow from Arendt, challenges the notion of the immortality of the group for which the leader serves as an emblem. Our collective closeness to death, exemplified by Biden, serves as a poignant reminder of our finitude and calls into question the republic's universal mortality.

It was Biden's age, verbal mishaps, and displays of confusion, all of which could have equally applied to his challenger, that drew scorn, mockery, and animosity from his opponents. For some, it appeared fairly impossible to fathom four more years of a Biden presidency because of projections of the precipitous decline of mental and physical capacities four years into the future. For others, it seemed nearly comical, baffling, absurd. And so, when absurdity becomes a Trojan horse for ideological rupture, laughter clears the ground for disbelief. By embellishing, mocking, and laughing at Biden's supposed incapacity, a response that became pervasive within MAGA circles, the possibility of the presidency being no longer animated by life but by decay became the lexicon of reactionary politics.

The enunciation of the necro-president materialized after the first and only debate between Biden and Trump, held on June 27, 2024. Following his disastrous performance, skeptics within the Democratic Party intensified pressure on Biden to withdraw from the race. Concerns about his age and the incoherent, meandering debate responses lent further credence to the framers' long-standing apprehension regarding older politicians.

In the wake of the debate, the concept of the necro-president took on a sharper definition and deeper resonance. On the second night of the Republican National Convention, July 16, 2024, Florida Governor Ron DeSantis delivered a sharp critique of Biden from the convention stage. DeSantis (2024) declared, "We need a commander-in-chief who can lead 24 hours a day, seven days a week. America cannot afford four more years of a *Weekend at Bernie's* presidency."[1] The reference to the 1989 film, in which two employees transport their deceased boss's corpse through a series of escapades, was not merely an attack on Biden's governance; there was much more to it. DeSantis boldly insinuated that a corpse now occupies the Oval Office. This portrayal extends beyond criticisms of ineffective leadership, advancing a more profound ideological claim: symbolically, Biden is *already* dead.

Following DeSantis's speech, *Politico's* Kimberly Leonard (2024) captured the thrust of this rhetoric: "He [DeSantis] said Biden was too feeble to discharge his presidential duties." Leonard's reporting brings us back to Hamilton's fears of a "feeble executive," underscoring the deeper issue: the mortal and existential legitimacy of Biden's presidency. The implication is clear. Biden's physical decline is not merely a matter of old age but a symbolic reflection of the presidency's broader decay.

The day after DeSantis's blistering comments, on July 17, White House Press Secretary Karine Jean-Pierre announced that President Biden had tested positive for COVID-19. As prominent megadonors and high-profile establishment leaders, such as Nancy Pelosi and Barack Obama, turned—privately and publicly—against Biden, the sitting president finally capitulated, bowing out of the race four days later on July 21 in a letter released on X, formerly Twitter (2024a; "Leaving the Race"). Thirty minutes later, Biden initiated a de facto procedural contingency by endorsing Vice President Kamala Harris (2024b; "Harris Endorsement"). Biden's preference for his replacement did not trigger a formal institutional realignment within the executive branch. Instead, it aimed to alleviate concerns and prevent a contentious convention fight within his party. The endorsement of Harris by Biden first, followed by other prominent Democrats, highlights the critical role of continuity in republican governance, whether maintained through codified governmental structures or informal processes.

The day after Biden's withdrawal from the race, DeSantis's portrayal of the necro-president from less than a week earlier was primed to explode across social media. Fueled by Alex Jones's (2024) seven-minute video titled "Is Joe Biden Dead?" theories affirming Biden's death spread rapidly across social media platforms. On X, more than 19 accounts actively perpetuated claims of Biden's death. Analyzing the breadth of these claims, Stuart Thompson (2024) of *The New York Times* writes, "Conversation about Mr. Biden on X that featured the word 'dead' or 'died' received nearly half a million mentions and more than four million interactions over a one-week period last month [July 2024] … Two of the most popular posts advancing the conspiracy theory together received more than 85 million views."

Prominent right-wing influencers played a crucial role in spreading these false claims. Stew Peters (2024) posted on X, "The real question is how long has Joe Biden been dead?"—a post that garnered over 47 million views. Popular podcaster Charlie Kirk (2024) tweeted, "Joe Biden was dying or possibly already dead," while

---

[1] See at the 00:59 mark.

Siraj Hashmi (2024) authoritatively declared, "Yeah, he's dead." Anarcho-capitalist writer and self-described troll Michael Malice (2024) chimed in, adding, "i [sic] mean, it's pretty much a given that Joe Biden is dead, right?" As the chorus of right-wing social media personalities unleashed tweet after tweet circulating claims of Biden's death, MAGA's most outspoken advocate followed suit.

Joining the fray was Colorado Representative Lauren Boebert (R), who issued a series of tweets in step with her fellow MAGA acolytes. "I demand proof of life from Joe Biden today by 5:00 pm," she insisted (2024b; "demand proof"). Even after Dr. Kevin O'Connor, Biden's physician, released a statement detailing the president's recovery and medical condition, Boebert doubled down: "A letter from a doctor is not proof of life. For the third time today, I'm asking Joe Biden to provide the American people with proof of life" (2024a; "not proof of life").

Although a recurring feature in American political discourse, this antagonistic, conspiracy-laden rhetoric takes on a more revealing dimension when considered alongside DeSantis's remarks. Both expose a fundamental belief that the occupant of the highest office in the land is *no longer alive*. To them, the corruption of liberal policies is so acute that the presidency is not merely controlled by the deep state or "postmodern neo-Marxists,"[2] to borrow a phrase from Jordan Peterson, but by the dead. DeSantis and Boebert's remarks point to a necrocracy—a government ruled by the dead, derived from the ancient Greek words *nekros* (corpse) and *kratos* (rule). In this vision, Biden is not merely a political adversary but the terminal embodiment of the presidency's decay. The office of the presidency has regressed into an empty place with death—both literal and symbolic—at its core, governed by the politics of entropy and decay.

While my framing of the necro-president focuses on the political and institutional implications of decay, it is critical to consider its cultural and psychological dimensions. Byung-Chul Han's *The Burnout Society* (2015) elucidates how late-capitalist societies, driven by an unyielding pursuit of productivity—what Han calls an achievement society—foster personal and collective exhaustion (8–11). Han argues that when pushed to its limits, exhaustion threatens to deplete individuals, collapsing institutions and society. This bio-level burnout, I suggest, also extends to political institutions, including those responsible for the continuation of the machinery of governance.

What begins as partisan theatrics—suggesting a corpse sits in the White House—soon transforms into a broader condition of governance itself, one marked by exhaustion, paralysis, and institutional decay. This erosion signifies the deterioration of individual agency and power, as well as the collapse of discursive and interpretative frameworks that once relied on a foundation that animated visions of institutional resilience and collective possibility.

The necro-president parallels Han's theorization of the achievement society by encapsulating a culture of overproduction and overexertion. This alignment

---

[2] The Living Philosophy. Postmodern Neo-Marxism—Jordan Peterson's Shadow [YouTube video], 25:24, February 7, 2022. https://www.youtube.com/watch?v=3kDpEKM7ZBI

4.1 "Proof of Life"

suggests that the presidency, much like society, has become a site where systemic burnout manifests in institutional paralysis, crisis, or, at its most extreme, death (Han, 2015, p. 51). The president no longer serves as a symbol of strength, longevity, or prestige but reflects an image of its fragility to society. Stripped of its veneer of greatness, the necro-president embodies a collective sense of powerlessness, frustration, and uncertainty, magnifying the broader anxieties of a faltering republic.

This corrosion of vitality in individuals and institutions is emblematic of a broader existential crisis within democracy itself. While Han's achievement society highlights the psychological and cultural tolls of overproduction and systemic exhaustion, Claude Lefort's analysis of modern democratic societies (1986) offers a critical lens for understanding the necro-president. Lefort argues that the diffusion of power in democracies creates an empty place (*lieu vide*)—a symbolic vacancy that resists permanent occupation.

Whereas Lefort sees this emptiness as precisely the safeguard of democracy, MAGA demands that it be filled—once and for all—with the figure of Trump. The necro-president reflects an inversion of Lefort's claim: the presidency becomes not a space of democratic circulation but a hollowed-out vessel overburdened by societal anxieties. In this symbolic seizure, MAGA reveals its anti-democratic agenda—what Lefort warns emerges whenever power seeks to permanently occupy the empty place, often leading to authoritarianism (1986, p. 303).

Lefort emphasizes that democracy is inherently characterized by indeterminacy, defined by the "dissolution of the markers of certainty" and the refusal to "occupy" the empty place of power (Lefort, 1988, p. 19). This indeterminacy enables democracy's open-ended and pluralistic nature, ensuring that no single figure or entity can fully embody power. Martín Plot argues that within the American republic, this site of power is increasingly "re-appropriated, in a more or less permanent fashion," through the conflation of "power, law, and knowledge" (2012, pp. 57 & 62).

In stark contrast to Lefort's interpretation, the MAGA movement rejects the emptiness ushered in by democracy, reframing Donald Trump as the ultimate eradicator of this emptiness. Trump's infamous assertion, "I have an Article II, where I have the right to do whatever I want as president,"[3] illustrates his expansionist interpretation of presidential powers, which he once described as akin to acting as a "dictator" but only on "day one" of his presidency.[4] His survival of two impeach-

---

[3] At a Turning Point summit in July 2019, Trump conflated the executive power enumerated in Article II of the Constitution with absolute authority. See Philip Bump, "Trump Falsely Tells an Auditorium Full of Teens That the Constitution Gives Him 'the Right to Do Whatever I Want,'" *The Washington Post*, July 23, 2019, https://web.archive.org/web/20190723232645/https://www.washingtonpost.com/politics/2019/07/23/trump-falsely-tells-auditorium-full-teens-constitution-gives-him-right-do-whatever-i-want/?utm_term=.5dec56cf3074

[4] In a December 2023 interview, Sean Hannity asked President Trump, "You are promising America tonight you would never abuse power as retribution against anybody?" Trump affirmed his commitment to upholding the rule of law, "*except for day one*" of his second administration (emphasis added). Following Hannity's praise, Trump posed a seemingly unthinkable question by most democratic norms: "You're not going to be a dictator, are you?" Leaning into the moment, Trump answered his own question with a rhetorical flourish, "No, no, no, other than day one." This

ment trials, coupled with his oft-repeated boast, "I could stand in the middle of Fifth Avenue and shoot somebody, and I wouldn't lose any voters" (Flores, 2016), underscores his ascendancy above the rule of law. Moreover, Trump has amplified his persona through grandiose declarations, referring to himself as a "very stable genius," further conflating his authority with intellectual and institutional supremacy (Colvin, 2018). Through this carefully curated framing, Trump is presented as a figure who transcends the temporal and institutional constraints of republican governance, anchoring the American nation-state within a voyage of divine providence. This foundationalist perspective situates the fulfillment of America's destiny as inseparably tied to Trump, portraying him as the singular figure capable of restoring order and purpose to a decaying political system.

4.2 "A Shield of Protection"

Just days after Biden's withdrawal, the necropolitical spectacle reached its apex—not in decay, but in divine resurrection. Following the July 13, 2024, attempted assassination at a rally in Butler, Pennsylvania, Trump's role ascended into the framing of a divinely chosen leader of the American people—an anointed servant of God tasked with securing the nation's survival. The assassination attempt represented more than mere opposition to Trump as an individual; it became a testament to his resilience and the enduring struggle against death itself. The survival of Trump explicitly functions as a mere political victory by carrying with it the implicit affirmation of divine appointment. His endurance serves as proof of the righteous significance of his mission.

As Secret Service agents were whisking away a bloodied Trump on the rally stage, he turned to the crowd, raised his fist, and proclaimed, "Fight, fight, fight," echoing his earlier call to "fight like hell" from four years earlier (Hutzler, 2023). The repetition of the word accentuates the moment's gravity, amplifying its connotation and imbuing it with a near-ritualistic quality.

By framing his survival as a political-spiritual victory, Trump weaves a narrative where death itself is not a threat but a backdrop against which his power is amplified. His survival of impending death becomes a rallying cry for the nation's soul, transforming a physical recovery into a symbol of national rebirth. The provocative content of Trump's message delivered a subliminal ultimatum: fight or die. To fight, in a Trumpian fashion, meant resisting the forces perceived as destroying the republic; it was to *wage war against death itself*. Trump's survival reinforced his perceived divine mission, suggesting that the republic's fate would be safeguarded

---

exchange encapsulated Trump's calculated embrace of authoritarian rhetoric, framing his potential actions on "day one" as an intentional exception to the democratic principles he otherwise professed to uphold. See David A. Graham, "Trump Says He'll Be a Dictator on 'Day One'," *The Atlantic*, December 6, 2023, https://www.theatlantic.com/ideas/archive/2023/12/trump-says-hell-be-a-dictator-on-day-one/676247/

under his leadership. The electoral choice became clear as common sense: life over death—Trump above all others.

For his supporters, Trump's survival was seen as divine intervention, aligning his purpose with God's plan. This developed into a central theme of the Republican National Convention, with its signs closely tied to the framing of Biden as a necro-president—a connection far from coincidental. And on the same night of the convention that saw DeSantis's Weekend at Bernie's analogy, former Housing and Urban Development Secretary Ben Carson articulated the antidote to the necro-president linked to Trump's vitality and ability to overcome decay. "I saw President Trump, a dear friend, escape death by mere inches," Carson eloquently stated, "And my thoughts immediately turned to the Book of Isaiah that says: 'No weapon formed against you shall prosper'" (Brown, 2024). In direct contrast to the necro-president, Carson portrayed Trump as not only surviving but as being shielded from death itself: "They tried to kill him, and there he is—alive and well. There's no doubt that God lowered a shield of protection over President Trump" (Brown, 2024). In this rhetorical framing, Trump is not merely a man who escaped minimally harmed; he is a vessel through which divine will flows, reinforcing the messianic narrative that elevates him beyond earthly limitations. His survival becomes a political rallying point and a metaphysical assertion of his right to lead.

On the convention's final night, prominent evangelist Franklin Graham, son of Billy Graham, opened the proceedings with a prayer. His introductory remarks were telling: "Last Saturday in Butler, Pennsylvania, President Trump had a near-death experience, no question. But God spared his life" (Rev.com, 2024). Merging the imagery of Christ's resurrection with Trump's messianic sheen, Graham suggested that "When President Trump *rose* from that platform, he *rose* with his fist raised in strength, showing America his unshakable resolve to fight for them and this nation" (Rev.com, 2024; emphasis added).

The various threads of this chronicle, from the putrefying Biden necro-presidency to Trump's perceived divine insulation from death, culminated in the pinnacle moment of the convention: the nomination acceptance speech. Continuing the theme of a protective divine shield, Trump asserted his belief that God was on "my side," adding, "I stand before you in this arena only by the grace of almighty God" (The New York Times). Honoring Corey Comperatore, who perished during the assassination attempt, Trump underscored the importance of sacrifice, mainly when it involves the ultimate cost of life. "There is no greater love than to lay down one's life for others," Trump offered (The New York Times). "This is the spirit that forged America in her darkest hours, and this is the love that will lead America back to the summit of human achievement and greatness. This is what we need" (The New York Times). Trump's rhetoric here moves beyond a simple political speech into the realm of spiritual warfare—equating his survival with a divine mandate to lead. The underlying message is clear. Trump is not just fighting for political power but for the very soul of America, positioning his leadership as a God-ordained mission to rescue a republic teetering on the brink of collapse.

What followed was remarkable and revealing. Trump's homage to fallen Americans seemed to suggest that countless sacrifices would be necessary to restore

America's greatness—death as a means of collective rejuvenation for the many, but not for Trump himself. By presenting himself as uniquely exempt from the finite nature of mortality and the decay that comes with it, Trump positioned himself as the *sole figure* capable of overcoming the necro-presidency and halting the national decline. "Nothing will stop me in this mission because our vision is righteous and our cause is pure," he asserted (The New York Times, 2024). Legal tribulations, assassination attempts, stolen elections, and even death itself were now recast as mere detours—some minor, others prolonged—in the resurrection of America as embodied by Trump.

In this logic, Trump positions death itself as a tool for mobilizing the electorate. The threat of death, both political and existential, works to unite his followers around a singular vision: the continued survival of the nation and the victory of Trump's divine leadership. He is not merely claiming to restore the country but reconstituting himself as the sole protector of the ultimate destruction.

The argument at play here is significant. As the necro-president, Biden is portrayed as incapable of fulfilling the presidency's stabilizing role within the republic, thereby hastening the collapse of the political system. The consequences are apocalyptic. The very fabric of republican history upheld through procedural contingency is now suspended while the condition of institutional inevitability accelerates unabated. Herein lies the grave threat. In line with Lefort, when power is no longer embodied in the presidency, it becomes ubiquitous, permeating down to the people and destabilizing the republican structure entirely.

For all the talk of Trump as a populist leader—and by logical extension, one who should welcome the return of power to the people—his rhetoric reveals a different story. As Savin and Treisman (2024) demonstrate in their meta-linguistic analysis, President Trump's speeches "contain fewer allusions to 'the people' than almost any other presidential candidate" (21), running counter to the traditional populist rhetoric in American history. More telling, however, is Trump's voracious attack on elites. Savin and Treisman show that since 1952, "no main party presidential candidate has made anti-elite references as persistently as Trump did in 2016, and his numbers remained high in 2024" (22).

Offering a qualitative assessment of public perceptions surrounding terms such as "the people" and "elites," DiMaggio et al. (2024) demonstrate how right-wing populism privileges projections of strong political leadership. Analyzing Harris Insights polling data of a nationally representative sample, they argue that populism relies on a cult of patriarchal personality, positioning Trump as a conduit for restoring power to "the people" while eliminating Democratic Party leaders alleged to be corrupt elites (106). Rooted in patriarchal dominance and racial purification narratives, right-wing populism rebukes not only corrupt actors but also the institutions in which they serve (101). The representative and governmental institutions conceptually collapse into a singular figure: a threat. This emphasis on attacking elites, rather than empowering "the people," *reveals a strategy not of democratizing power but of consolidating it*. Trump's rhetoric resonates with regimes that wield power through control—of bodies, speech, and even death itself.

The notion of "divine protection" becomes weaponized in Trump's narrative—a shield that serves to protect the individual and reinforce his transcendence over mortal limits. By aligning his survival with divine will, Trump fortifies his position, signaling to his followers that he is above and beyond the inevitable decay of the republic.

Speaking to the fascist and authoritarian aspects of Trump's leadership and his ability to rally support, Ruth Ben-Ghiat argues that since 2015, Trump "has been conditioning [his supporters] to see other Americans as enemies, as diseased, as dirty" (PBS NewsHour, 2024). This process of othering, targeting groups ranging from migrants to leftists to LGBTQIA+ persons, reveals how the specter of death operates within republican governance. At the same time, ostensibly anathema to the principles of republicanism, the use of death as a tool to neutralize external and internal threats becomes an essential mechanism for consolidating power. Ben-Ghiat (2022) makes a similar point, observing, "Over time, the political system increasingly reflects the personal values and mission of the personalist leader—and that usually means the institutionalization of thievery, lying, and repression" (25). A critical extension of Ben-Ghiat's analysis is warranted to account for the institutionalization and instrumentalization of death, not only as a physical threat but as a symbolic force capable of shaping political meaning and sustaining power.

When these discursive choices are examined alongside the concept of the necro-president, Trump emerges in a new mold: a divinely anointed leader, chosen by God and the American people, tasked with keeping power away from elites and opposition forces to save the republic from impending doom. Conversely, the continuation of a necro-president would precipitate the ruination of once-great governing structures, where chaos—a primordial, quasi-state of nature—reigns supreme.

4.3 A Surrogate of Death

Following Biden's departure from the race in late July, Trump shifted tactics to link his new challenger, Vice President Kamala Harris, to a decaying administration. The strategy played out on two fronts. First, by tying Harris to Biden, Trump drew a direct line from what he called Biden's failures—on immigration, the economy, and global conflicts—to what he claimed would be the inevitable outcome of a Harris presidency. He portrayed her as a radical leftist and a continuation of the same broken system. The message was clear: nothing would change, and everything would get worse. In this narrative, Harris isn't just another opponent. She's a stand-in for institutional rot, the figure through which decay continues. Trump's attack isn't only about policy; it's about survival. Harris represents the lingering death of a political order that, in his view, was already in freefall.

The second front went deeper, building on Trump's long-running attacks on Biden's age and mental decline. With Biden out, Trump redirected that anxiety toward Harris. It wasn't just that Biden had failed. His presence, and now his absence from the race, symbolized something much gloomier: death entering the political sphere. What began as a critique of competency turned into something more symbolic. In this version of the story, Harris inherits not just the office, but the death drive attached to it.

Trump cast her not just as weak but as carrying a political death sentence, linked to a presidency that no longer works or lives. For Trump, her campaign didn't promise a fresh start; it advanced the slow unraveling of the republic.

At his first rally, after Biden dropped out, Trump made this case more explicit. He accused Harris of hiding Biden's cognitive decline, claiming she had helped cover it up (The Daily Star, 2024). "Kamala Harris knew all along about Joe's problems, and she chose to hide it from the American people. Is this who we want leading our country?" he asked a crowd in Charlotte, North Carolina (Touchberry et al., 2024). Others echoed the charge. Representative Mike Lawler (R-NY), for example, accused Harris of "gaslighting" the public (Touchberry et al., 2024). This wasn't just about dishonesty. The accusation positioned her as someone propping up a failing system, preserving the illusion that the presidency was still functioning. Harris was suddenly inadvertently cast as the protagonist for a redux version of *Weekend at Bernie's* responsible for dragging her boss's corpse all around the executive branch and campaign trail.

During the September 10 debate between Harris and Trump, the image of the necro-president returned, this time in an even more surreal form. When asked about the war in Ukraine, Trump said, "And we have a president that we don't even know if he's—where is our president? We don't even know if he's a president." As moderator David Muir attempted to step in, Trump continued, "We have a president who doesn't know he's alive" (ABC News, 2024).

The comment was absurd but sharp. Trump took the idea of Biden as the necro-president and pushed it further. Biden isn't just dead politically—he doesn't know whether he's alive. It's a bizarre inversion of the *The Sixth Sense*. In the film, Bruce Willis's character is dead and doesn't realize it until the end. Trump flips it. Biden thinks he's dead, but no one seems to notice, and everyone keeps pretending the system is working.

That move does more than mock Biden. It throws the entire idea of a stable political reality into question. If the president can be alive and dead, if the office can function and fail simultaneously, then what exactly are we witnessing? This isn't just political critique. It's a breakdown of shared reality giving way as the spectacle consumes the real. And, truth, now subsumed by power, becomes liquefied into an empty signifier, devoid of mutual understandings of objectivity, malleable and amorphous enough to assume myriad epistemological masks, disguising submission as freedom, the fantastical as the real.

But, this is where Trump's rhetoric becomes stranger and even more dangerous. It's no longer about *who governs* but whether governance still holds any meaning at all. The question isn't just whether Biden is fit for office but whether the office itself is receptive to any form of life.

The Sixth Sense asks a haunting question, perhaps more apropos now than at its release: how would we know if we were already dead? Trump hijacks that question and points it at Biden, turning him into the ghost of a republic that's been in decline for years. In this collapse of certainty, where spectacle and reality blur, the president becomes a kind of quantum figure, alive and dead, depending on who's watching and what version of the truth they've come to believe. Trump turns the collapse of truth, reason, objectivity, democratic norms inter alia into a rallying cry. Biden doesn't just represent failure but the quintessential embodiment of a republic in decay. And Trump, once again, positions himself as the only one who can bring it back to life.

Trump's association of Harris with the specter of the necro-president narrative peaked in October, just weeks before the general election. During a widely criticized appearance on *The View*, Harris was asked what she would have changed about the past three and a half years of the Biden presidency. Her response: "There is not a thing that comes to mind" (Nava, 2024). Harris's reply, even for supporters, came off as flat and out of touch. Seizing on the moment, the Trump campaign launched a series of targeted ads focused on key swing states like Arizona, Georgia, Michigan, North Carolina, Nevada, Pennsylvania, and Wisconsin—all of which Trump would go on to carry weeks later. By amplifying the gaffe, Trump doubled down on his portrayal of Harris as incapable and out of step, positioning her as the continuation of the decay that began under Biden.

The ads were sensational and ominous, depicting a Harris presidency as more of the same: more weakness, more war, more welfare for "illegals," more taxes. One ad ended with the statement: "Nothing will change with Kamala" (Nava, 2024). While overblown rhetoric is nothing new in US campaign ads, this one echoed Trump's necro-presidency narrative. Paired with his earlier *Sixth Sense*-style jabs at Biden, the suggestion that Harris represents "nothing" reinforces the image of a presidency hollowed out by death, decay, and stagnation. In this frame, Harris isn't just a candidate—she becomes the ultimate symbol of political entropy. "Nothingness" becomes a political attack and a metaphysical claim: she doesn't just lack vision or leadership. She is the void itself, an absence where political life once thrived during a golden past.

The ad's emphasis on nothingness is particularly potent. It alleges a lack of effective governance and the absence of stability and order. As the inheritor of Biden's legacy, Harris is portrayed as presiding over a future administration trapped within a prolonged funeral oration for the necro-president in a dying republic. A requiem for the necro-president of the past and a reconstitution of death assuming a new corporeal form for the present serve as first-order principles of a Harris regime. The inability to act, the failure to govern effectively, and the persistence of dysfunction are presented as the inevitable future under Harris's surrogacy.

Yet, in this narrative of nothingness, Trump's campaign offers a contrasting vision: a possibility for restoration. By claiming that the republic could reanimate *ex nihilo* through his victory, Trump positioned himself as the sole figure capable of reviving a decaying republic and steering it away from the abyss. This contrasts with the vision of death under Biden and Harris with the promise of life under Trump. The republican ideal of renewal, rebirth, and vitality is reimagined through Trump's rhetoric: his victory is not just about reclaiming power but saving the republic from itself, transforming the election into an existential battle over the very survival of the American experiment in self-government.

Viewed through this lens, the 2024 presidential election assumes unprecedented significance. It transcends the usual contest for electoral gains and control of federal offices, emerging as a struggle over life and death—for the presidency and the republic itself. Rather than rejuvenating the republic, Biden's presidency—and, by extension, Harris's campaign—carries with it a fatal assurance of an accelerated demise in the worldview of MAGA. The fragility of Biden's presidency mirrors the fragility of the republic itself.

In her work *On Violence* (1970), Hannah Arendt explores the profound relationship between institutions and the people's ability to perceive them as vibrant and vital. Expounding on the necessity of this "livingness" to sustain institutions, Arendt writes: "All political institutions are manifestations and materializations of power; they petrify and decay as soon as the living power of the people ceases to uphold them" (41). Procedural safeguards that once protected the system have eroded, transforming the presidency into a necrocratic institution. Yet, Arendt's diagnosis is correct, albeit in reverse: it is not the people's withdrawal of power that has drained vitality from the presidency, but the institution itself that has become devoid of life, prompting a corresponding withdrawal of popular support. In this manner, a vote for Trump must be seen as an affirmation of life—an ontological struggle to revive the republic.

4.4 The Specter of Death

The influence of the dead within governing structures is not unique to the MAGA imagination. The relics of the deceased have long shaped political systems. The deification of pharaohs in ancient Egypt, rulers under China's Mandate of Heaven, and Roman emperors established enduring legacies that shaped successive generations, ensuring a sense of continuity between past and present. In his "Theses on the Philosophy of History" (1968), Walter Benjamin postulates that the dead exert influence over present political structures, reminding us that history is often written under the weight of the past's unfulfilled promises. Benjamin writes, "In other words, our image of happiness is indissolubly bound up with the image of redemption. The same applies to our view of the past, which is the concern of history. The past carries with it a temporal index by which it is referred to as redemption. There is a secret agreement between past generations and the present one" (254). Benjamin emphasizes the link between present-day understandings of the conditions of social life and the relation to historical ideals that shape such perspectives. This cuts to the central contradiction of the American republic, embodied in the guiding principle of "all men are created equal" enshrined within the Declaration of Independence. Here, the promise of equality and freedom is prefigured within the historical contradictions of its inception.

The promise of a republic that embodies these ideals has always been haunted by the failure to fully deliver on it. This ongoing unfulfilled promise fuels and exacerbates political tensions within the contemporary American landscape. As we observe

4.4 The Specter of Death

the growing tension between Trump's vision and the decaying remnants of a democratic republic, the specter of a broken promise lingers, serving as a paradoxical foundation for the necro-president.

The redemptive promise of the Declaration has historically been housed within the framework of the presidency as an institution symbolic of the republic's capacity to deliver on such grand ideals. However, the erosion of the presidency's capacity—its transformation into a necrocratic institution—suspends the teleological unfolding of these ideals. Benjamin's assertion that the present is responsible for fulfilling the aspirations of the past reveals the profound inadequacy of the slogan "Make America Great Again." Instead of a return to past greatness, it signifies the need to wholly and finally reconcile with the deferred promises of the past. Yet, the specter of the necro-president disrupts this "secret agreement" between past and future, interrupting the esoteric transmission of generational aspirations and achievements. Instead, the figure of the necro-president acts not only as a reflection of institutional decay but also as a vehicle through which these unfulfilled promises are both resurrected and distorted. In a sense, Trump's appeal to past greatness is an attempt to take hold of the unfinished narrative of American history, offering a false redemption rooted in nostalgia rather than racial or social progress.

Benjamin's notion of "weak Messianic power" becomes pivotal here. He writes, "Like every generation that preceded us, we have been endowed with a weak Messianic power, a power to which the past has a claim. That claim cannot be settled cheaply" (254). This is the crux of Benjamin's claim regarding messianic power: Trump's careful self-depiction as the redeemer of a declining republic exploits the symbolic weight of this power. The 2024 election exemplifies this dynamic. Within this framework, the figure of Trump ascends to a messianic role—not merely as a political contender but as a redemptive figure, offering the promise of reviving a republic on the brink of collapse. His candidacy reflects both a desperate bid for vitality and a longing to return to an imagined past—a past now overshadowed by the haunting specter of its decline.

Yet, this desire for a return—the yearning to reach back to a time that never truly existed as depicted in its idealized form—underscores the precariousness of Trump's claim to be the nation's savior. His messianic rhetoric is a redemptive figment, an attempt to fabricate a past that will never come to fruition despite the earnestness of his followers. In doing so, he becomes trapped by the very history he seeks to revive, bound by the contradictions of the republic's fractured legacy.

Benedict Anderson's (1983) concept of imagined communities is useful here to illustrate how shared histories and myths, often tied to national figures, shape norms of societal cohesion by fostering a collective sense of belonging and purpose. Nations, Anderson argues, are socially constructed through shared symbols, narratives, and rituals that bind individuals into a common identity, even among those they will never meet (6). Ceremonies, institutions, and a perceived collective destiny sustain these imagined communities, and leaders often serve as focal points for their shared mythos. For example, figures like Abraham Lincoln or Franklin D. Roosevelt have come to embody resilience, unity, and the aspirational ideals of the American republic. Yet, as Anderson warns, when these figures or the institutions they represent lose their outward projections of strength and legitimacy, the cohesion of the imagined community begins to unravel (36).

The unraveling of the imagined community under Trump becomes evident in the increasing polarization and mythologizing of historical figures. While Trump may present himself as the leader who will "reclaim" and "restore," he simultaneously deepens the fissures between different articulations of American identity, disintegrating the shared narrative of the republic and replacing it with a fractured, divisive myth of return to a community and for white Christian nationalists.

The presidency, once a unifying force and sovereign embodiment of the imagined community of the American republic, now faces a crisis of legitimacy. Its capacity to unite opposing constituencies has eroded, weakening public trust, collective identity, and a shared purpose. This fragmentation creates an opening for alternative narratives to reconstitute the imagined community of the American "people," often by exploiting lines of racial, ethnic, and gendered exclusion. Trump, in particular, has capitalized on this fracturing, deepening cultural, economic, and social cleavages while positioning himself as a panacea for the republic's ailments. His rhetoric and governance style draw on nostalgia for an idealized past, offering the illusion of unity while intensifying the divisions within the nation sans stable channels conducive to the translation of conflict into political freedom and equality for all.

In this sense, Trump's ability to manipulate the political discourse hinges on his capacity to capitalize on the imagined history of the republic, retooling it to serve his divisive narrative. The concept of "unity" becomes a rhetorical device, used strategically to consolidate his power and reframe the "decay" of American democracy due to the liberal establishment, migrants who are "poisoning the blood," radical intellectuals inter alia rather than an intrinsic feature of republican governance itself.

Jacques Derrida's hauntology concept further points to death's efficacy within a social imagination, exploring how the dead—or the lingering presence of the past—continue to shape contemporary institutions and discourse. In *Specters of Marx* (1994), Derrida writes, "The specter is a paradoxical incorporation... something that is not present in flesh and blood, but it weighs on the present, it inscribes itself there, and it continues to return" (4–5). Derrida argues that haunting goes beyond mere remembrance or commemoration; it actively disrupts and shapes the present. The specter of the past exposes the incomplete foundations of our systems—politically, linguistically, and institutionally—highlighting the unfulfilled promises that underpin them. Returning to Benjamin's concept of the "secret agreement" and Anderson's idea of the fragmented community, haunting reveals, in the margins of visibility, how institutions, symbols, and language—ranging from governance to religion—are not only materially constructed but also critically erected on the unrealized promises of the past. Derrida's hauntology underscores a view of politics as architecture—an ongoing process of constructing the systems we inhabit, yet one constrained by the designs imbued with the unrealized promise of the past.

Derrida's concept of haunting serves as a critical lens through which to view the decay of American democratic structures under Trump. The specter is not simply a ghost of the past; it is actively shaping and distorting the present, just as Trump's vision of America summons a mythologized past while disregarding the inherent contradictions of the republic's foundation. This haunting complicates the tale of America's greatness, turning the figure of the necro-president into the embodiment of both past promises and present decay.

4.4 The Specter of Death

Trump's use of language and style of governance, shaped by the pursuit of "greatness" embedded in the slogan "Make America Great Again," amplifies this haunting by resurrecting the past as an episteme for organizing the present. The past not only lingers as a specter but also problematizes the ability of present-day institutions to govern effectively, as they remain deeply tied to interpreting the original design. For the framers of the Constitution and MAGA supporters, the presidency was envisioned as an active force—embodying life and death within the republic. Yet, it has become haunted and depleted, leaving nothing more than an empty shell of what it once symbolized.

This hollowed-out figure—the necro-president—becomes a synecdoche for the republic, seemingly suspended between life and death. The presidency, once a force for national unity and vision, now exists as a spectral echo of its former self, manipulated by figures like Trump to achieve a vision of American "greatness" that cannot ever fully materialize but continues to circulate with the nation's fractured imagination.

While reverence for the dead is common in social groups, the current sociopolitical moment reveals a rupture: the denial of reverence for the dead stems from the fact that death itself has infiltrated the institutional edifice of governance. No longer confined to the symbolic figure of a leader, death has permeated the very architecture of the republic, eroding its legitimacy and vitality. The presidency, once a symbol of collective strength and renewal, now reflects the frailty of the institutions it represents. What is at stake is not merely the survival of a leader but the survival of the republic itself. Trump does not simply emerge as a political contender but assumes a messianic role—a symbolic savior offering the promise of revival to a republic critically on life support.

But here lies the paradox of Trump's necro-president narrative: the republic is doomed and in need of rescue, requiring a savior to delay its inevitable collapse. Trump's intervention is framed as critical because death has already infiltrated the republic's institutions, accelerating its destruction. His rhetoric, primarily targeting a white nationalist Christian electoral base, reimagines the biblical story of the Fall of Man as an allegory for the American republic. Central to this retelling is the inevitability of human failure, postulating that salvation lies beyond the temporal realm of politics or history.

In a critical point of return, this interpretation carries with it Augustine's dichotomy between the City of God and the City of Man. The figure of Trump as a messianic savior of the republic carries enormous implications. If the republic were somehow saved from its inevitable demise, as MAGA adherents believe, a transformative revision in the history of republican tradition would transpire: the creation of a *permanent republic*. Trump alludes to this permanence, telling Christian voters that if they vote for him "in four years, you don't have to vote again" (Reid, 2024). The elimination of the necessity of the vote suggests that decline has been suspended—that the symptomatic anxieties endemic to republics have been resolved. A return to power for Trump would signal the ultimate overcoming of institutional inevitability and procedural contingency conditions. The history of the American republic would separate itself from the history of all previous regimes, free from the *logic of inevitable demise*. A conquering of time, placing the American republic outside the cycle of birth, decay, and death common to all prior republics, commences. A Trumpian republic signifies the complete restoration of the potential greatness of the American republic, fully and finally realized in the present moment—a specific event universalized.

Yet, a permanent republic anchors the City of Man to a temporal existence, an earthly dwelling. The architecture of the permanent republic would be solidified in the *here and now*, erasing the indeterminacy of man and the predestination of God's plans through a resolution of eschatological implications. Such a creation would resist the natural forces of decay and time and safeguard itself against human vices. The transubstantiation of the decaying republic into a permanent republic presupposes that the sinful nature of man—the mark and consequence of the Fall—has been somehow resolved. Soteriological authority becomes vested within the republic itself, not outside of it, suggesting that a messianic Trump would preempt Christ's ability to return and redeem the faithful. Man is, thereby, reborn and transformed into a higher order—a recalibration of virtue perfectly aligned with an ethic of greatness that is the rightful providential gift of the American people.

The American republic, in this vision, appears as the exclusive home for "real Americans," necessitating a purge of those whose political ideology, race, ethnicity, language, or sexuality indicate incompatibility (Johnson, 2019). This is the purpose of weaponizing the Department of Justice against political opponents, initiating the "largest domestic deportation operation in American history," and eroding bodily autonomy (Savage et al., 2023). The arrival of the permanent republic under Trump offers a reclaiming of what is believed to *rightfully belong to the republic*, actualized within the domain of the executive: the power to regulate life and death. It culminates in the ultimate triumph over internal institutional death, embodied in the spectral figure of the necro-president.

But all of this—a permanent republic, a rebirth of the American people, a purge of those antithetical to the new order—stands in opposition to the catalog of religious, political, and moral beliefs held by many MAGA adherents. To act in pursuit of the permanent republic is to undermine the Christian promise of eternal salvation prophesied through the *return* of the messiah rather than in the *arrival* of a permanent earthly republic. Salvific habitation is not worldly; it lies in a different kingdom, not of man but of God.

The permanence of a Trumpian republic is irreconcilable with the permanence of a spiritual kingdom. Trump, therefore, cannot fully embody a messianic role unless one truly believes he is the messiah, for which, then, institutional collapse becomes imminent. For MAGA supporters, this, of course, creates a profound contradiction: an elevation of Trump as a messianic figure endowed with the talents to rescue the republic while simultaneously preparing it for divine fulfillment. But to preserve the republic indefinitely undermines the telos of its destined collapse, forcing supporters to place their faith in earthly permanence rather than divine providence.

In doing so, they risk becoming what they most despise—idolaters worshiping a worldly figure through a rejection of the unfolding of God's plan. Unless, of course, one is to truly believe Donald J. Trump *is* God.

References

Anderson, B. (1983). *Imagined communities: Reflections on the origin and spread of nationalism*. Verso.
Arendt, H. (1970). *On violence*. Harcourt Brace.
Ben-Ghiat, R. (2022). Strongmen: The politics of domination. *New Republic, 253*(5), 25.
Benjamin, W. (1968). Theses on the philosophy of history. In H. Arendt (Ed.), *Illuminations: Essays and reflections* (pp. 253–264). Schocken Books.
Biden, J. (@joebiden). (2024a, July 21). Harris endorsement. *X*.
Biden, J. (@joebiden). (2024b, July 21). Leaving the race. *X*.
Boebert, L. (@laurenboebert). (2024a, July 22). A letter from a doctor is not proof of life. *X*.
Boebert, L. (@laurenboebert). (2024b, July 22). I demand proof of life from Joe Biden today by 5:00 pm. *X*.
Brown, J. (2024, July 17). Dr. Ben Carson quotes Isaiah during RNC speech, says God shielded Trump from death. *The Christian Post*. https://www.christianpost.com/news/ben-carson-quotes-isaiah-during-rnc-speech-says-god-saved-trump.html
Colvin, J. (2018, January 6). Trump says he's 'like, really smart,' 'a very stable genius'. *AP News*. https://apnews.com/article/2bb960fda0264c488d454632628cb193
DeSantis, R. (2024). Ron DeSantis speaks at RNC 2024 night two. *Rev*. https://www.rev.com/blog/transcripts/ron-desantis-speaks-at-rnc-2024-night-two
DiMaggio, A., Wahlrab, A., & Ochs, H. (2024). White supremacy and the January 6 insurrection: Mass opinion and the mainstreaming of 'Great Replacement' theory. *Populism, 7*(1), 106–127.
Flores, R. (2016, January 23). Donald Trump: 'I could shoot somebody and I wouldn't lose any voters'. *CBS News*. https://www.cbsnews.com/news/donald-trump-i-could-shoot-somebody-and-i-wouldnt-lose-any-voters/
Han, B.-C. (2015). *The Burnout Society* (E. Butler, Trans.). Stanford University Press.
Hashmi, S. (@SirajAHashmi). (2024, July 22). Yeah, he's dead. *X*.
Hutzler, A. (2023, July 17). 'Fight, fight, fight' has become an RNC rallying cry under Trump. *ABC News*. https://abcnews.go.com/Politics/fight-fight-fight-become-rnc-rallying-cry-trump/story?id=112027742
Johnson, T. R. (2019, July 16). Trump's 'real Americans' are white and Christian. *The Guardian*. https://www.theguardian.com/commentisfree/2019/jul/16/trump-real-americans-white-christian
Jones, A. (@RealAlexJones). (2024, July 22). Is Joe Biden dead? *X*.
Lefort, C. (1986). In J. B. Thompson (Ed.), *The political forms of modern society: Bureaucracy, democracy, totalitarianism*. MIT Press.
Lefort, C. (1988). *Democracy and political theory*. University of Minnesota Press.
Leonard, K. (2024, July 17). Ron DeSantis says Joe Biden isn't the nominee but a 'puppet' for the far left. *Politico*. https://www.politico.com/live-updates/2024/07/17/rnc-live-updates-coverage/ron-desantis-joe-biden-nominee-00168977
Malice, M. (@michaelmalice). (2024, July 22). I mean it's pretty much a given that Joe Biden is dead, right? *X*.
Nava, V. (2024, October 16). Trump campaign releases new ad centered on Kamala Harris telling 'The View' she'd do 'not a thing' different than Biden. *New York Post*. https://nypost.com/2024/10/16/us-news/trump-campaign-releases-new-ad-centered-on-kamala-harris-telling-the-view-shed-do-not-a-thing-different-than-biden/
ABC News. (2024, September 10). Harris vs. Trump Presidential Debate: Transcript. *ABC News*. https://abcnews.go.com/Politics/harris-trump-presidential-debate-transcript/story?id=113560542
PBS NewsHour. (2024, October 28). How Trump's rhetoric compares to historic fascist language. *PBS*. https://www.pbs.org/newshour/show/how-trumps-rhetoric-compares-to-historic-fascist-language
Peters, S. (@realstewpeters). (2024, July 22). The real question is how long has Joe Biden been dead? *X*.

Plot, M. (2012). Lefort and the question of democracy—In America. *Constellations, 19*(1), 57–70.

Reid, T. (2024, July 28). Trump tells Christians they won't 'have a vote' after this election. *Reuters*. https://www.reuters.com/world/us/trump-tells-christians-they-wont-have-vote-after-this-election-2024-07-27/

Rev.com. (2024). Franklin Graham speaks at RNC 2024, night four. *Rev*. https://www.rev.com/transcripts/franklin-graham-speaks-at-rnc-2024-night-four

Savage, C., Haberman, M., & Swan, J. (2023, November 11). Sweeping raids, giant camps and mass deportations: Inside Trump's 2025 immigration plans. *The New York Times*. https://www.nytimes.com/2023/11/11/us/politics/trump-2025-immigration-agenda.html

Savin, N., & Treisman, D. (2024). Donald Trump's words. *NBER Working Paper*, No. 32665, 1–30.

The Daily Star. (2024, July 25). Trump calls Kamala Harris a 'lunatic' at first rally after Biden's exit. https://www.thedailystar.net/news/world/usa/news/trump-calls-kamala-harris-lunatic-first-rally-biden-exit-3661781?amp

The New York Times. (2024, July 19). Trump RNC Speech Transcript. https://www.nytimes.com/2024/07/19/us/politics/trump-rnc-speech-transcript.html

Thompson, S. A. (2024, August 7). What do conspiracy theorists do when proved wrong? Double down or move on. *The New York Times*. https://www.nytimes.com/2024/08/07/technology/biden-conspiracy-theories-misinformation.html

Touchberry, R., Schilke, R., & Bullis, H. (2024, July 23). Republicans say Harris was complicit in shielding Biden's cognitive decline. *Washington Examiner*. https://www.washingtonexaminer.com/news/3095140/republicans-harris-complicit-shielding-biden-cognitive-decline

Open Access This chapter is licensed under the terms of the Creative Commons Attribution 4.0 International License (http://creativecommons.org/licenses/by/4.0/), which permits use, sharing, adaptation, distribution and reproduction in any medium or format, as long as you give appropriate credit to the original author(s) and the source, provide a link to the Creative Commons license and indicate if changes were made.

The images or other third party material in this chapter are included in the chapter's Creative Commons license, unless indicated otherwise in a credit line to the material. If material is not included in the chapter's Creative Commons license and your intended use is not permitted by statutory regulation or exceeds the permitted use, you will need to obtain permission directly from the copyright holder.

Chapter 5
Pace Death

To philosophize is to learn how to die.
Michel de Montaigne

Abstract In this chapter, I argue that the fantasy of a permanent American republic is central to the necro-political condition. From executive orders to campaign rhetoric, Trump's aesthetic project attempts to construct a vision of national permanence through architecture, symbolism, and spectacle. These efforts reanimate fascist imaginaries under the guise of national renewal, framing political decay as divine restoration. I argue that death is no longer understood as the republic's eventual limit but is absorbed into its governing logic, shaping how permanence, power, and legitimacy are imagined. I advance an ethic of acting with death as a way to confront decline, not as failure, but as a condition of political life. This commitment insists on the urgency of building differently, inhabiting collapse without replicating it, and imagining life within and against the inevitability of loss.

Keywords Necro-politics · Trumpism · Fascist aesthetics · Political resistance · Political mourning · Political imagination · Political aesthetics · Architecture and power

Republican theory has long taught that all republics are mortal, destined to collapse under the cruel fate of time. Today, the American republic stands at a critical threshold where decay and nostalgia collide, reanimating fascistic impulses in dangerous ways. The MAGA movement, asserting that the forces of death have infiltrated the institutions meant to preserve the republic, positions itself as the antidote to this decline. Yet, its proposed solution—rebuilding America through mythic ideals of greatness, reminiscent of a twenty-first century Tower of Babel—reveals its dangerous fascist imaginary.

In the final days of his first term, Trump sought to reshape the nation's aesthetic and symbolic identity through Executive Order 13967: Promoting Beautiful Federal Civic Architecture (Federal Register, 2020). By elevating classical architecture as the only legitimate style for federal buildings, Trump denounced modernist designs as symbols of disorder, fragmentation, and moral decay. His scorn for "ugly buildings" and exaltation of neoclassical grandeur reflected a paleoconservative disposition hostile to the secular, scientific, and modern. Architecture became a political weapon, erecting structures that embodied tradition, power, and the mythic stability of a republic perceived to be under siege.

Biden's revocation of the order in February 2021 (Federal Register, 2021) sharpened cultural and political divisions between institutionalists and reactionaries and the tableaus of modernity and nostalgia. As part of his 2024 presidential platform, Trump revitalized the debate over architectural control offered in his Agenda 47 by proposing the creation of ten "freedom cities" (Trump, 2023). These cities, he claimed, would reopen the American frontier, invoking Manifest Destiny and national rejuvenation. Yet, beneath the rhetoric of renewal lies a haunting familiarity: the fascist impulse to reterritorialize space as a means of erasing the present and imposing a mythologized order into the future.

In his second inaugural address, Trump framed his return to the presidency as nothing short of a metaphysical restoration. Declaring that the "decline is over," Trump positioned himself as the singular force capable of reversing America's decay (2025). The speech, steeped in messianic rhetoric, suggested that he had been "saved by God to make America great again," casting his political survival and reelection as divinely ordained. In his words, January 20 became "Liberation Day," a symbolic break from what he described as the tyranny of the past four years. "The revolution of common sense" has begun, Trump declared, evoking fascistic motifs to signal a return to truth, strength, and national purpose. "The future is ours, and our golden age has just begun," he concluded, blending eschatology and nationalism into a civil theology in which time, history, and destiny all converge in him.

On the same day after being sworn into office, Trump recommitted to architectural mastery by issuing a new memorandum, Promoting Beautiful Federal Civic Architecture. The memorandum directs the General Services Administration to prioritize classical architectural styles for all future federal buildings (White House, 2025). Framed as a return to "dignified" civic spaces, the memorandum extended Trump's architectural imaginary into a second term, emphasizing neoclassical design as the preferred expression of national unity, strength, and beauty. While legally mundane, the directive reaffirms the fascistic totalization of space, memory, and materiality. Codifying nostalgia into physical structures reifies a vision of Trump's republic as immutable, orderly, and sacred. Such architecture strips the socialness of public space, reshaping it as a tribute of permanence intended to outlast those of the present.

The parallels to Mussolini's fascist cities—constructed to exalt the grandeur of Imperial Rome—are inescapable. Throughout the late 1920s and early 1930s, Mussolini reclaimed Italy's swamplands to build Littoria, Carbonia, and Guidonia, cities that exemplify fascist renewal and the reterritorialization of national grandeur

(Nicoloso, 2022). Trump appropriates this impulse through his invocation of the "swamp." No longer a physical terrain, the swamp functions as a metaphor for decay—a space that must first be purged to permit rebirth. Much like Mussolini's reclamation projects, Trump's freedom cities rise from the ruins, enclosing the swamp as a site of the profane and a fertile ground for sacred revival.

Yet, as with Mussolini, Trump's vision privileges style over inhabitation. His rejection of "ugly buildings" reflects a deeper fascistic instinct to control not just the aesthetics of space but its meaning, reducing architecture to a symbolic assertion of order, tradition, and permanence. Asserted as beautification, the demand for an architectural cleanse reveals a profound hostility toward a perceived belief in modernity's spiritual indeterminacy and moral chaos. Trump's vision imposes a rigid, nostalgic ideal that erases the complexity of communal belonging, replacing it with performative grandeur through an architecture of spectacle and death.

First as Tragedy, then as Farce At its core, the architectural battle mirrors the broader necropolitical crisis facing the American presidency. Once a symbol of institutional resilience, the presidency has become a site of fragility, decay, and symbolic death. Critics framed Biden's presidency as emblematic of institutional collapse, amplifying public anxiety. The repeated question in the years, months, and weeks in the run-up to the 2024 election by pundits and voters alike—"Is Biden too old to lead?"—was ultimately a diversion. The real issue was perceiving his physical fragility as symptomatic of a republic teetering on the edge of viability.

As we saw in the previous chapter, this anxiety boiled over during Lauren Boebert's absurdist demand for "proof of life," a moment initially dismissed as political theater yet disturbingly significant. The grotesque call to affirm Biden's life reflects a latent collective fear to prove its leader and institutions remain alive. To demand evidence of life is to acknowledge the specter of death implicitly. Boebert's rhetoric transcends partisan theatrics, exposing the hollowness of a system *performing life* even as its institutions, symbols, and culture visibly erode.

In the aftermath of Kamala Harris's electoral defeat, New York Governor Kathy Hochul's remarks further underscore the absurdity and tragic necessity of proving life within our necropolitical condition. At a post-election meeting of Democratic governors, where Biden's age dominated discussions, Hochul quipped, "When I was growing up, people who were 65 were almost dead. I'm 65. I'm not almost dead" (Glueck et al., 2024). Beneath the farcical tone of these comments, there lies a telling admission. The truth that is contained within Hochul's words denies the absurdity of its exposition, in that the necropolitical order requires continual proof of life precisely to mask its ongoing decline—*pace death*. Hochul's insistence on vitality serves less as a personal defense and more as a diagnosis of a faltering system obligated to announce its vigor through increasingly despondent performances of life.

From Democrats to Republicans—and those in between—many questioned whether Biden was too old for a second term, although he is only three years the senior of Trump. Nevertheless, prominent party leaders and talking heads stressed that his deteriorating cognitive and linguistic functions could hinder effective governance and lead America into a period of critical decline. These questions and concerns made sense, yet they only perpetuated the current order of what is possible. The response we should have collectively offered concerning Biden's age was: "*So what?*"

This response would have been helpful—not as a defense of Biden's candidacy or an endorsement of his first term—because it requires us to consider where politics can and should go in today's perilous times. If one were to truly trust the Madisonian system, then the occurrence of an actual death of a sitting president would have been sufficiently dealt with by the succession plan. However, fears concerning the possibility of Biden's death while in office are less about the viability of lines of continuity and more of a collective unease over what the proximity of presidential death would mean for the republic as a whole. The inability to delineate the *death of one* from the *death of all* is the inescapable mark of the necropolitical condition.

Act with Death We must *act with death*—whether perceived in the domain of the executive, in the disintegration of public trust, or the systemic erosion of democratic norms—*and collapse*—whether within the courts, culturally, or structurally—because it is *already occurring*. To act with death is to recognize the magnitude of our actions in the present, to affirm both our individual and collective mortality, and to thoughtfully consider how, where, and in what ways our decisions inflict indefensible, unmitigated harm on others. I propose that a phenomenology of foretold death is thus to pace intentionally, acknowledging how individual and social destruction is not an anomaly but a condition. This is partly to take Hannah Arendt's (1998) insight seriously that death is not simply an end but a condition of natality, the ever-present backdrop against which political action gains urgency, unpredictability, and meaning. To act with death is to affirm that the possibility of beginning anew resides precisely in the shared experience of unknown finitude.

What it does not mean is descending into nihilism nor reacting with terroristic intent but embracing the challenge of building new structures—new forms of architecture that may exist, at times, within and, perhaps in the future, outside of—the current design of possibility. Urgently erecting new spaces that challenge the tectonic architecture of the republic offers a poetic reminder of our natality and how the actions of the present may one day haunt the future—if there is to be one at all. *Not just pace death but embrace death.*

The presidential election of 2024 reveals the ongoing existential crisis of the American republic, forcing us to confront whether it can (or should) be rescued or if it has reached the inevitable end of its life cycle. The endeavors to defeat the necro-president and the jubilant *fait accompli* of the conquering of death offer a warning. In a society where death is regulated and instrumentalized, where can we erect public spaces of intimate co-habituation, action, and mourning? Here, we must think of the incarcerated person sentenced to die in a space designed against inhabitation, intended for the administration of death. The prisoner's fate is a quiet death devoid of publicness, with mourning rendered possible only in the quiet cracks of social life. We must ask ourselves: what other spaces and institutions—beyond the prison—have been erected for death at the expense of life?

Giorgio Agamben observes that "architecture is the art of building, insofar as it is also the art of inhabitation" (Agamben, 2018). A permanent Trumpian republic entwines a fascistic foundation in a redemptive, salvific, messianic fashion. Through the defeat of the necro-president, life is assumed to have triumphed; yet, without death, life loses its social character, erasing the horizons of memory and remembrance. Life sans death is predicated upon an anti-socialness that lingers within an architecture *contra* inhabitation, leaving the inevitability of loss as an indistinguishable note. It becomes life without possibility, devoid of the indeterminacy of the future.

The History of Republics Has Taught Us Otherwise A permanent republic cannot endure. The fallibility and vices of its people, the accumulation of wealth into fewer hands, the subversion of justice, and the hubris of its leaders will eventually bring the entire tower crashing down. The death of the American republic, once unimaginable, is no longer a question of *if* but *when*. What architectural ruins will serve as the obituary of the American republic? In the spaces of political imagination—institutional, symbolic, and spiritual—the clash for the republic's future will continue to unfold in a thousand unexpected ways.

References

Agamben, G. (2018, December 7). *Inhabiting and Building*. Lecture delivered at the Faculty of Architecture, University of Rome. https://illwill.com/inhabiting-and-building

Arendt, H. (1998). *The human condition*. University of Chicago Press. (Original work published 1958).

Executive Office of the President. (2020). Executive order 13967 of December 18, 2020, "Promoting beautiful federal civic architecture". *Federal Register, 85*(247), 83589–83592. https://www.govinfo.gov/content/pkg/FR-2020-12-23/pdf/2020-28605.pdf

Executive Office of the President. (2021). Executive order 14018 of February 24, 2021, "Revocation of certain presidential actions". *Federal Register, 86*(38), 11855–11856. https://www.federalregister.gov/documents/2021/03/01/2021-04281/revocation-of-certain-presidential-actions

Glueck, K., Epstein, R. J., & Corasaniti, N. (2024, December 9). How old is too old to be president? Democrats still don't want to say. *The New York Times*. https://www.nytimes.com/2024/12/09/us/politics/president-age-democrats.html

Nicoloso, P. (2022). *Mussolini, architect: Propaganda and urban landscape in Fascist Italy* (S. Notini, Trans.). University of Toronto Press.

Trump, D. J. (2023, March 3). *A new quantum leap to revolutionize the American standard of living*. https://www.donaldjtrump.com/news/2b9c56eb-718a-4420-86fd-34dc330b65a5

Trump, D. J. (2025, January 20). *The inaugural address*. The White House. https://www.whitehouse.gov/remarks/2025/01/the-inaugural-address/

White House. (2025, January). Promoting Beautiful Federal Civic Architecture. https://www.whitehouse.gov/presidential-actions/2025/01/promoting-beautiful-federal-civic-architecture/

Open Access This chapter is licensed under the terms of the Creative Commons Attribution 4.0 International License (http://creativecommons.org/licenses/by/4.0/), which permits use, sharing, adaptation, distribution and reproduction in any medium or format, as long as you give appropriate credit to the original author(s) and the source, provide a link to the Creative Commons license and indicate if changes were made.

The images or other third party material in this chapter are included in the chapter's Creative Commons license, unless indicated otherwise in a credit line to the material. If material is not included in the chapter's Creative Commons license and your intended use is not permitted by statutory regulation or exceeds the permitted use, you will need to obtain permission directly from the copyright holder.

The manufacturer's authorised representative in the EU is Springer Nature Customer Service Centre GmbH, Europaplatz 3, 69115 Heidelberg, Germany. If you have any concerns regarding our products, please contact ProductSafety@springernature.com

Printed and bound by CPI Group (UK) Ltd, Croydon, CR0 4YY

23/03/2026

02076398-0012